FACES OF THE FEW

The Battle for Survival in the Summer of 1940

FACES OF THE FEW

The Battle for Survival in the Summer of 1940

Dilip Sarkar MBE FRHistS

AIR WORLD

AIR WORLD

FACES OF THE FEW
The Battle for Survival in the Summer of 1940

First published in Great Britain in 2023 by
Air World
An imprint of
Pen & Sword Books Ltd
Yorkshire – Philadelphia

ISBN 978 1 39906 536 8

Typeset by SJmagic DESIGN SERVICES, India.

Printed and bound in the UK by CPI Group (UK) Ltd.

Pen & Sword Books Limited incorporates the imprints of Atlas, Archaeology, Aviation, Discovery, Family History, Fiction, History, Maritime, Military, Military Classics, Politics, Select, Transport, True Crime, Air World, Frontline Publishing, Leo Cooper, Remember When, Seaforth Publishing, The Praetorian Press, Wharncliffe Local History, Wharncliffe Transport, Wharncliffe True Crime and White Owl.

For a complete list of Pen & Sword titles please contact

PEN & SWORD BOOKS LIMITED
47 Church Street, Barnsley, South Yorkshire, S70 2AS, England
E-mail: enquiries@pen-and-sword.co.uk
Website: www.pen-and-sword.co.uk

Or
PEN AND SWORD BOOKS
1950 Lawrence Rd, Havertown, PA 19083, USA
E-mail: Uspen-and-sword@casematepublishers.com
Website: www.penandswordbooks.com

MIX
Paper | Supporting
responsible forestry
FSC® C013604

Contents

Introduction   vi

Faces of The Few   1

Acknowledgements   206

Bibliography   207

Other books by Dilip Sarkar   208

Introduction

What was the 'Battle of Britain'?

Having finally attacked the West on 10 May 1940, ending months of so-called 'Phoney War', Germany's shocking, lightning-quick, advance to the Channel coast was both unprecedented and unexpected. The Netherlands, Belgium and Luxembourg were rapidly overwhelmed, the British Expeditionary Force suffering the ignominy of being evacuated from the French port of and beaches around Dunkirk. On 22 June 1940, France surrendered, leaving Britain alone to defy Hitler. To the shores of the 'Sceptred Isle' came men from Britain's Empire and Commonwealth, and those from the occupied lands determined to continue the fight. With the United States still neutral, it was imperative that Britain remained free, in the hope that eventually, with American aid, the liberation of Nazi dominated Europe could be launched from the ports of southern England. Hitler, however, was suddenly presented with an opportunity to mount a seaborne invasion of south-east England – but first required control of the air. Britain was defended by Royal Air Force Fighter Command, which, during sixteen blood-stained weeks of high summer and autumn, successfully fought off the Luftwaffe's determined attacks – thus keeping Britain in the war and preserving this essential base. This epic aerial conflict became known as the Battle of Britain.

Who were 'The Few'?

On 20 August 1940, the British Prime Minister, Winston Churchill, immortalised the young RAF aircrew of Fighter Command when he described them as the 'Few' – who, at the time, were still fighting against overwhelming odds. Over eighty-years later, fascination with that legendary summer endures, and the Few, of course, are centre-stage.

After the Second World War was won, the crucial importance of the Battle of Britain was recognised by the Battle of Britain Clasp to the 1939-45 Star, awarded to the Few. To qualify, the member of aircrew concerned must have flown at least one operational patrol between 10 July 1940 and 31 October 1940, with one of the officially accredited Fighter Command and associated units considered to have fought the battle. Nearly 3,000 such aircrew received the coveted Clasp. There was, however, no similar recognition for the aircrew of Bomber Command, who had contributed by, amongst other things, attacking the enemy invasion preparations, or Fighter Command's support staff. Furthermore, aircrew who had given their lives defending Britain but not serving with one of the officially recognised Fighter Command units also went unrecognised – which is somewhat unfair, considering that not all of the Few actually saw action during the Battle of Britain. Be all of that as it may, though, as its title indicates, this book is exclusively concerned with the Few themselves.

Why are these photographs special?

Understandably, during the Second World War unofficial photography was prohibited on service installations. Nonetheless, a surprising number of candid, amateur, snapshots were taken, which, although lacking the clarity and composition of the official pictures, provide us an authentic record and window through which we can still peer at the distant past. It was always these photographs, usually taken on comparatively primitive equipment, rather than the oft-published official pictures, that interested me, and my close relationship with many of the Few provided a unique opportunity to examine their personal albums, copying and collating snapshots of interest. Some survivors had but a handful of pictures, others none at all, whilst a small number had weighty albums full of precious images. The thing that stood out from nearly all of these collections was that their content was predominantly images of people – not aircraft. That suited me perfectly, because primarily my personal interest has always been in the human experience and stories of the people involved. A selection of these photographs appears in the following pages, along with some official images, privately commissioned studio portraits, and amateur photographs taken of the Few in later life. Collectively, these photographs provide a unique and personal record of some of the Few I once knew, or some of those who either perished during the Battle of Britain or before the war's end. Indeed, the collection emphasises the uncertainty of life during the Battle of Britain and beyond, and equally just how many aircrew were amateur volunteer reservists or auxiliaries – without whom Fighter Command could not possibly have successfully defended Britain in 1940.

So, welcome to, and I hope you enjoy, 'Faces of the Few'…

Dilip Sarkar MBE FRHistS, 2022

Faces of The Few

The photograph which so inspired me as a child. Taken at Fowlmere, the Duxford satellite airfield, by official Air Ministry and award-winning press photographer Stanley Devon on the evening of 21 September 1940, this haunting image shows Squadron Leader Brian Lane DFC (centre), the commander of 19 Squadron (centre), with his 'A' Flight commander, Flight Lieutenant Walter 'Farmer' (or 'Jack') Lawson DFC (left) and Flight Sergeant George 'Grumpy' Unwin DFM shortly after landing from a patrol over London at 25,000 feet. No enemy aircraft were encountered during this sortie, during which Lane actually led the five-squadron strong 'Big Wing'. Lane was an exceptional fighter pilot and leader who was sadly shot down by Oberleutnant Walter Leonhardt off the Dutch coast and reported missing on 13 December 1942. Lawson, who later commanded 19 Squadron, was similarly lost without trace when shot down over Rotterdam on 28 August 1941. Of the three, only Unwin survived the war, a tough and aggressive fighter ace who remained in the post-war service and saw further action in Malaya. Perhaps the most remarkable thing about this famous image is that it appears the photographer himself was unaware of just what an iconic photograph he had taken.

Although Devon's photographs taken at Fowlmere are well-known, other photographs of Squadron Leader Lane are extremely rare. This studio portrait originated in his widow's estate and shows Brian as a young pilot officer before the war.

Above: After the Battle of Britain, in June 1941, Squadron Leader Lane left 19 Squadron and served on the HQ staff of RAF Middle East. During that deployment he managed to do some flying, and is seen here in desert uniform before returning home due to ill-health in 1942. This image was also discovered in his widow's estate.

Right: Walter Lawson pictured as a pre-war sergeant-pilot flying Hawker Fury biplane fighters with 43 Squadron at Digby (Trevor Lawson).

Above: Another of Devon's Fowlmere images, Flight Sergeant Unwin with his Alsatian, 'Flash'.

Opposite above: In 2006, the author persuaded die-cast model manufacturer Corgi to produce a model of one of Grumpy's Spitfires, QV-H, P9546. Wing Commander George Cecil Unwin DSO DFM is seen here at home in Ferndown, Dorset, with the resulting model, shortly before his death, aged 96, on 28 June 2006. The author was particularly close to George and was honoured to speak at his friend's funeral.

Opposite below: Another 19 Squadron pilot photographed by Devon was Pilot Officer Richard Jones, who had previously flown Spitfires with 64 Squadron at Kenley in 11 Group. Richard later became a test pilot and survived the war, ultimately working as a court usher.

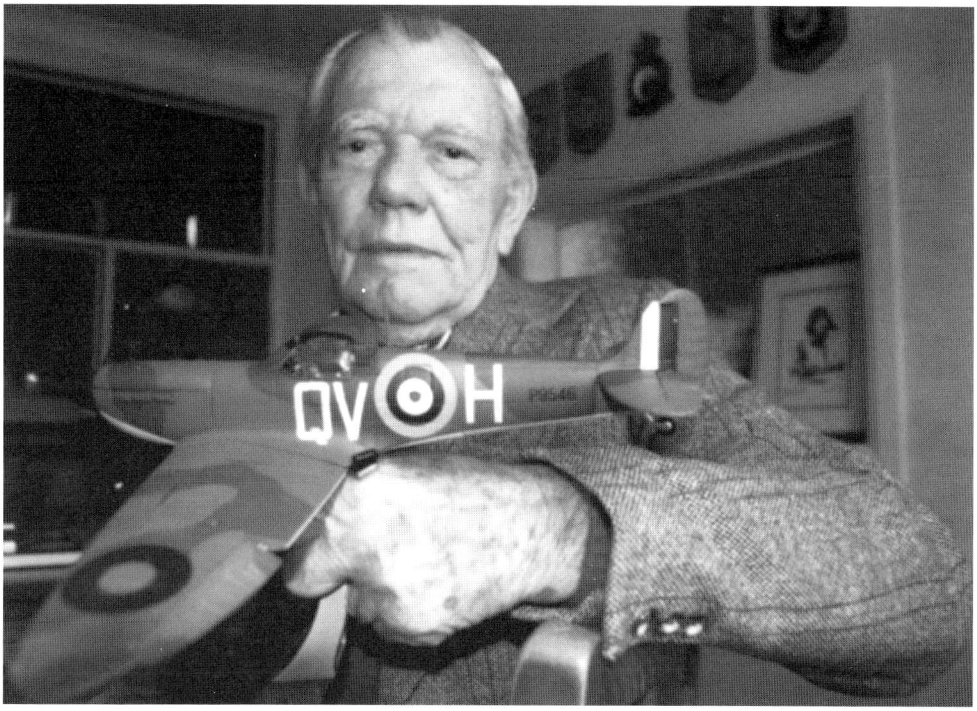
QV
H

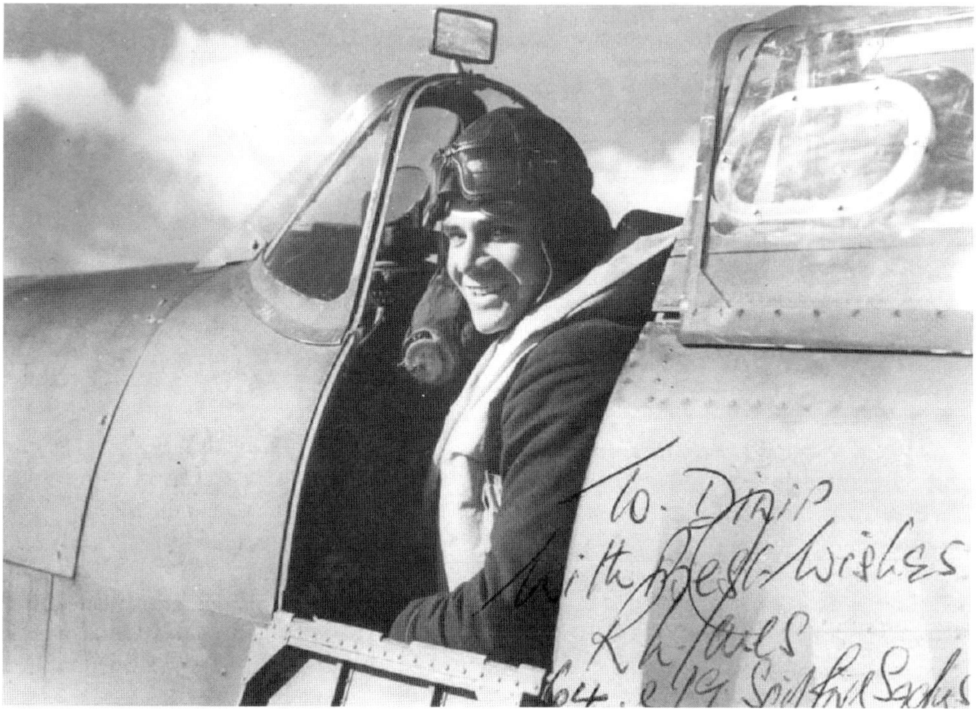
With Best Wishes

Above: Flight Lieutenant Richard Jones photographed at home in Witney, Oxfordshire, by the author in 1992. Richard had only recently seen the famous Devon photograph for the first time at a car boot sale, and promptly bought it! He died on 9 March 2012.

Opposite above: Another iconic Devon Fowlmere photograph, showing armourer Fred Roberts re-arming the guns of Sergeant Bernard 'Jimmy' Jennings' Spitfire QV-I, X4474. A posed image, Jennings had just landed having 'beaten up' the airfield for the photographer's benefit.

Opposite below: In 1992, Wing Commander Bernard Jennings AFC DFM (left) and Fred Roberts were reunited in Great Malvern at the launch of the author's book *The Invisible Thread: A Spitfire's Tale*. The Spitfire behind them, although a Mk XVI, was painted to represent X4474.

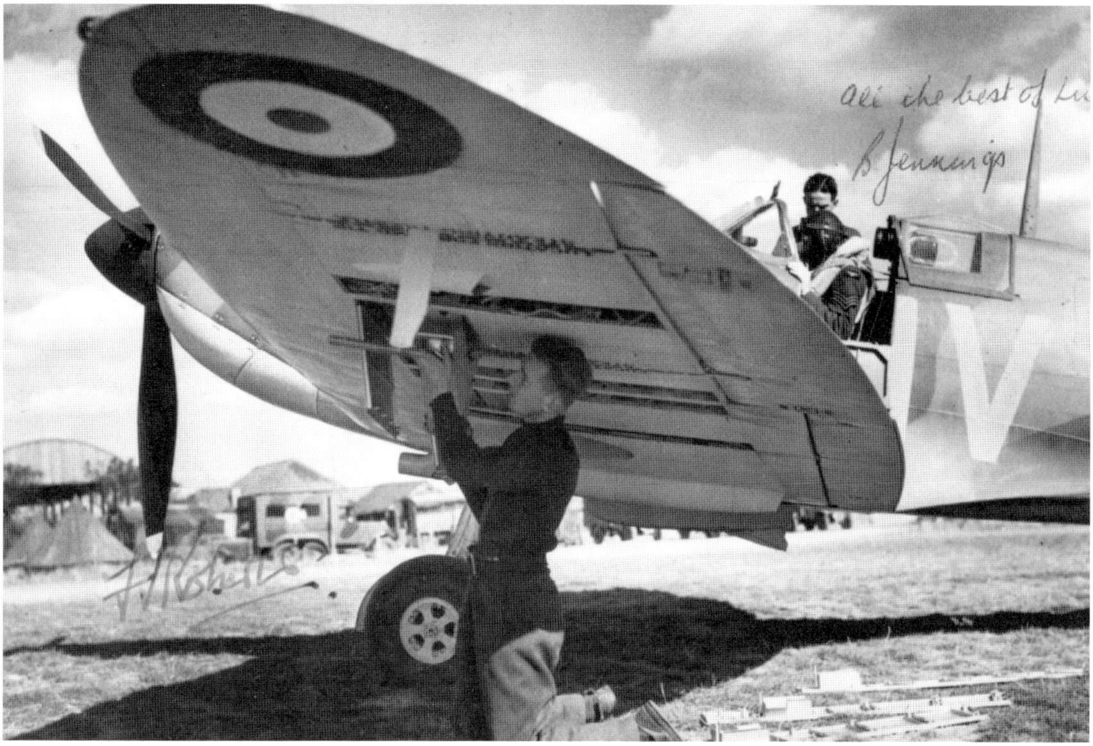
all the best of lu
B Jennings

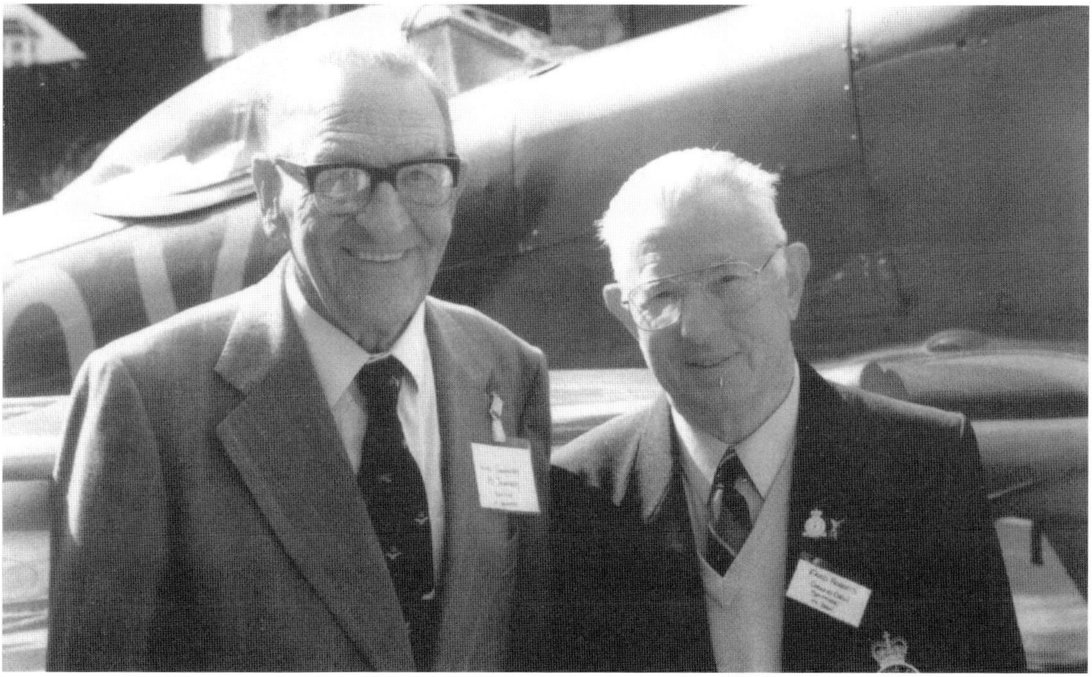

Above: Yet another superb Devon image, this being Pilot Officer Wallace 'Jock' Cunningham DFC, also of 19 Squadron.

Opposite: Flight Lieutenant Cunningham was shot down by ground fire and captured during the same operation in which Squadron Leader Lawson was reported missing. He is pictured here on 8 May 1945 with a model of Spitfire P9546, which he also flew, presented at the launch of the author's book *A Few of the Many*, held at Worcester Guildhall.

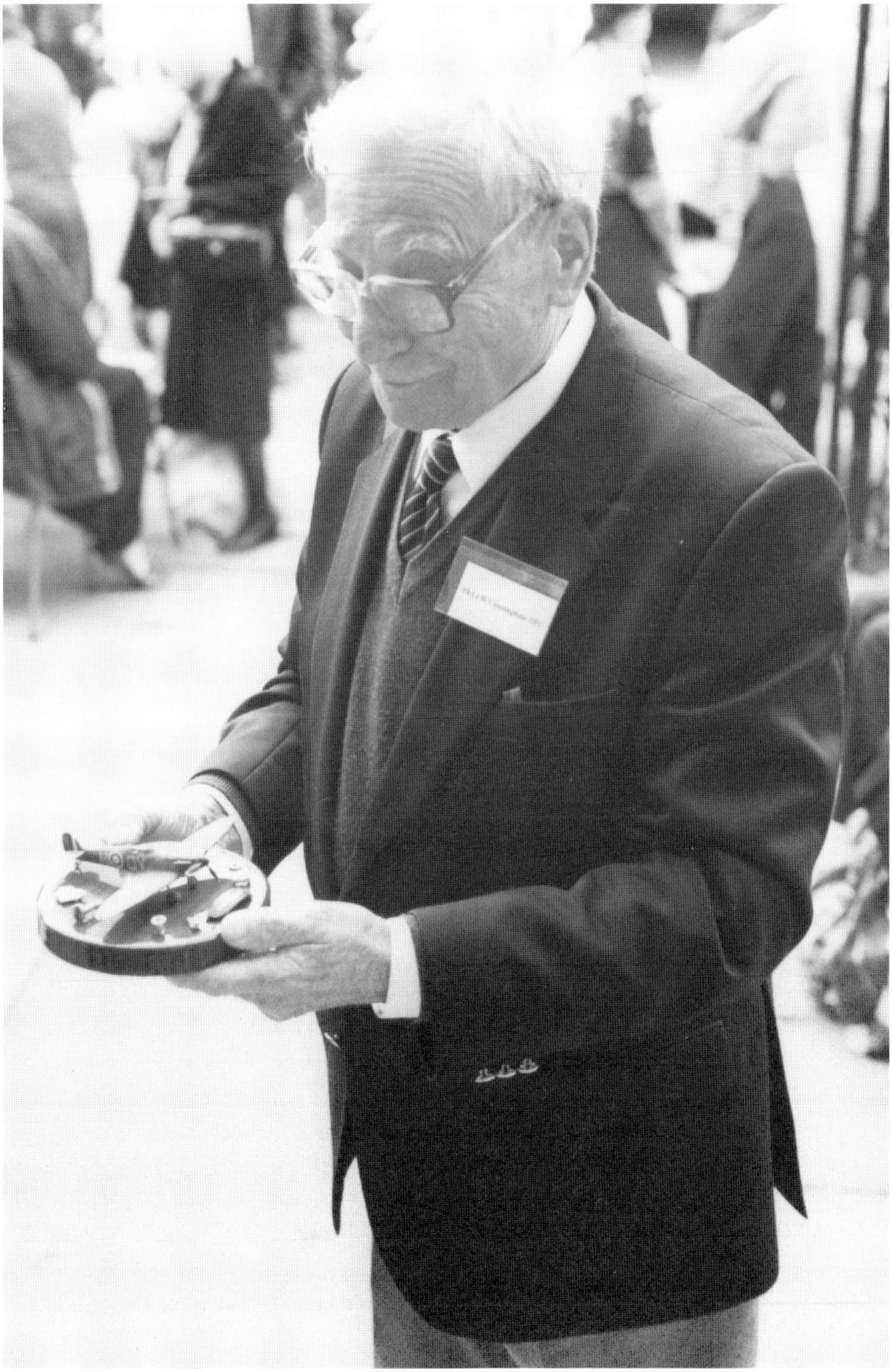

Two 92 Squadron fighter aces at Biggin Hill: Flight Lieutenant Brian Kingcome DFC and Pilot Officer Geoffrey 'Boy' Wellum DFC, the latter being only 18 during the Battle of Britain. In 2002, Geoff's memoir, *First Light*, became a best-seller and is rightly recognised as a classic.

Above: Squadron Leader Wellum also saw action over Malta, and after various appointments, including a spell as a test pilot at Gloster Aircraft, remained in the post-war RAF. In retirement he lived in Cornwall, a keen ship modeller, and was photographed at home in 2014 by the author for inclusion in *The Final Few*. Geoff died on 18 July 2019.

Right: Sergeant Frank Twitchett flew Hurricanes with 43 and 229 Squadrons during the Battle of Britain, before flying Spitfires with 145 Squadron and participating in the Non-Stop Offensive of 1941, flying from Tangmere. On 21 June 1941, Frank's Spitfire was badly damaged when attacked over the Channel by Oberleutnant Matzke of II/JG 26, but he made it home. He later flew Spitfires in the Middle East and survived the war.

Flight Lieutenant Frank Twitchett pictured with poet and re-enactor Larry McHale at a Battle of Britain symposium hosted by the author at Worcester Guildhall in 1998. Sadly, Frank died in November of that year.

Sergeant Bill Green with his beloved wife, Bertha. Bill first joined the Auxiliary Air Force as a fitter in 1936, and was fortunate to become a fighter pilot. Flying Hurricanes with 501 Squadron, he was shot down on 29 August 1940, baling out at 16,000 feet – his parachute only opening at 300 feet. Having narrowly escaped death, Bill survived the war.

Flight Lieutenant Bill Green pictured at home by the author in 2014, for inclusion in *The Final Few*. Sadly, Bill died on 7 November that year, so did not live to see the book in which his story was told.

Above: Gordon Batt, a volunteer reservist, hailed from Coventry and destroyed several enemy aircraft during the Battle of Britain whilst flying Hurricanes with 238 Squadron. He later flew Typhoon fighter-bombers and survived the war.

Left: Flight Lieutenant Gordon Batt was a popular guest at the author's many book launches and other events, until his death on 4 February 2004.

Michael Wainwright learned to fly pre-war with the Civil Air Guard before taking a Short Service Commission in 1937. Flying Spitfires with 64 Squadron, Michael destroyed a 109 over Dunkirk during Operation DYNAMO, and shared the destruction of another during the Battle of Britain. He survived the war and eventually retired as a squadron leader decorated with the Air Force Cross.

Above: Squadron Leader Michael Wainwright pictured at home in Stourbridge, Worcestershire, by the author in 2014, during the course of research for *The Final Few*. Sadly, Michael was another contributor who did not survive to see the book published – he died on 23 March 2015.

Opposite: Wing Commander John Francis Durham Elkington – universally known as 'Tim' – was a Cranwellian who flew Hurricanes with 1 Squadron at Northolt during the Battle of Britain. Having destroyed a 109 on 15 August 1940, the following day he was shot down over Portsmouth by the German ace Major Helmet Wick. Although wounded, Tim baled out safely (a story in itself) and did not fly operationally again until October. He remained convinced that had this not been the case then, owing to his inexperience, he would not have survived the heavy fighting of September. After many other narrow escapes and service overseas, Tim remained in the post-war service, flying many aircraft types, including the four-engine Avro Shackleton, eventually retiring in 1975 to run a picture framing business.

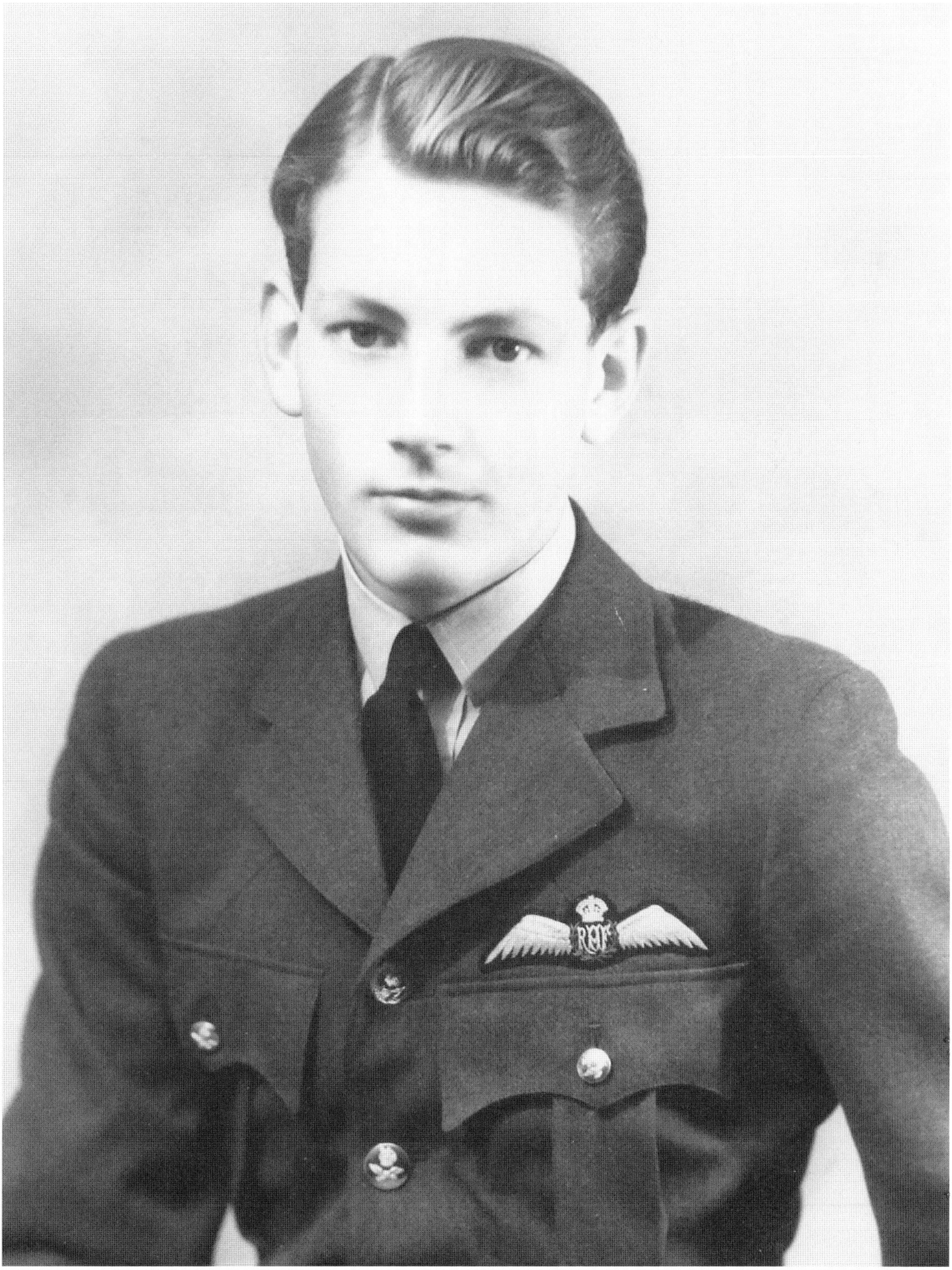

Wing Commander Tim Elkington pictured at home in Little Rissington, Gloucestershire, by the author whilst researching *The Final Few*, in 2014. An extremely modest man who refused to accept the view that he had ever done anything extraordinary, his story was told, in his own words and for the only time, in that book. Tim left us on 1 February 2019, aged 98, and the author was honoured to speak at this remarkable man's memorial service.

Group Captain Tom Gleave was a pre-war pilot flying Hurricanes with 253 Squadron at Kenley, who claimed five Me 109s destroyed on 30 August 1940, making him an ace in one day, although only one was confirmed whilst the others were recorded as 'probables'. The following day, Gleave was shot down in flames and horrendously burned, subsequently receiving reconstructive treatment at the Royal Victoria Hospital, East Grinstead, from the plastic surgeon Sir Archibald McIndoe. It was there that with other aircrew patients he became a founder member of the exulted 'Guinea Pig Club'. As 'Chief Guinea Pig', Gleave devoted much of his life to assisting fellow 'Pigs'. Eventually, he returned to duty, commanding RAF Manston during both the 'Channel Dash' and Dieppe operations. In 1941, his Battle of Britain memoir, *I Had A Row With A German*, was published – in 2021, his original manuscript, entitled *Nemesis of Eagles,* was discovered and at the time of writing is currently being prepared for publication by Pen & Sword.

Above: Group Captain Tom Gleave CBE was invalided out of the RAF in 1953, after which he became a full-time Cabinet Office historian, working on the official histories of the Second World War. For some years, Tom served as historian to the Battle of Britain Fighter Association, until his death in 1993. His detailed story is told in full in the author's *Forgotten Heroes of the Battle of Britain* (published by Pen & Sword in 2022).

Opposite: Peter Hairs was a pre-war volunteer reservist who joined 501 'County of Gloucester' Squadron, flying Hurricanes, at Tangmere in January 1940. He saw action in both the Fall of France and Battle of Britain, claiming victories, after which he served as a flying instructor at home and abroad. He left the service as a flight lieutenant in 1945, having been made a Member of the Most Excellent Order of the British Empire (MBE) in recognition of his wartime efforts.

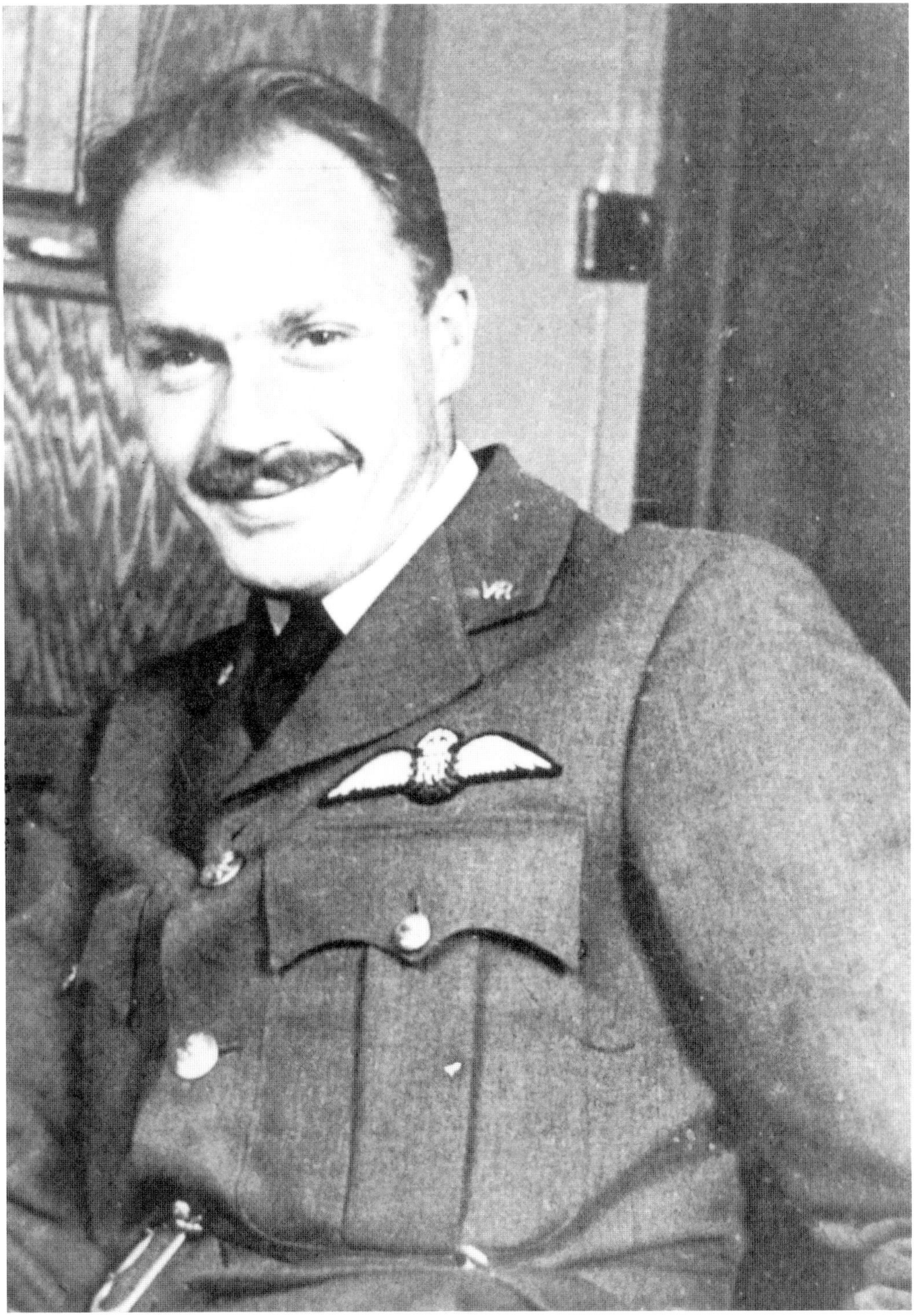

Above: After the war, Peter Hairs became a bank manager and Justice of the Peace, and is pictured here before returning to the skies in a Tiger Moth shortly before his death, aged 99, on 24 August 2014.

Opposite: Peter 'Sneezy' Brown took a Short Service Commission in 1938, and during the Battle of Britain flew Spitfires with both 611 Squadron as a part of the 12 Group Duxford-based 'Big Wing', and 41 Squadron in 11 Group. He claimed a number of aerial victories, including the Me 109 of 5/JG 52's Feldwebel Bielmaier over West Malling on 20 October 1940. The German pilot was captured and Pilot Officer Brown visited his vanquished foe in the 'lock up'. The pair shook hands and Peter took Bielmaier's *schwimmveste* as a souvenir, the German life jackets being far superior to the RAF's 'Mae Wests'. Peter is pictured here wearing his highly prized trophy at Hornchurch in early 1941.

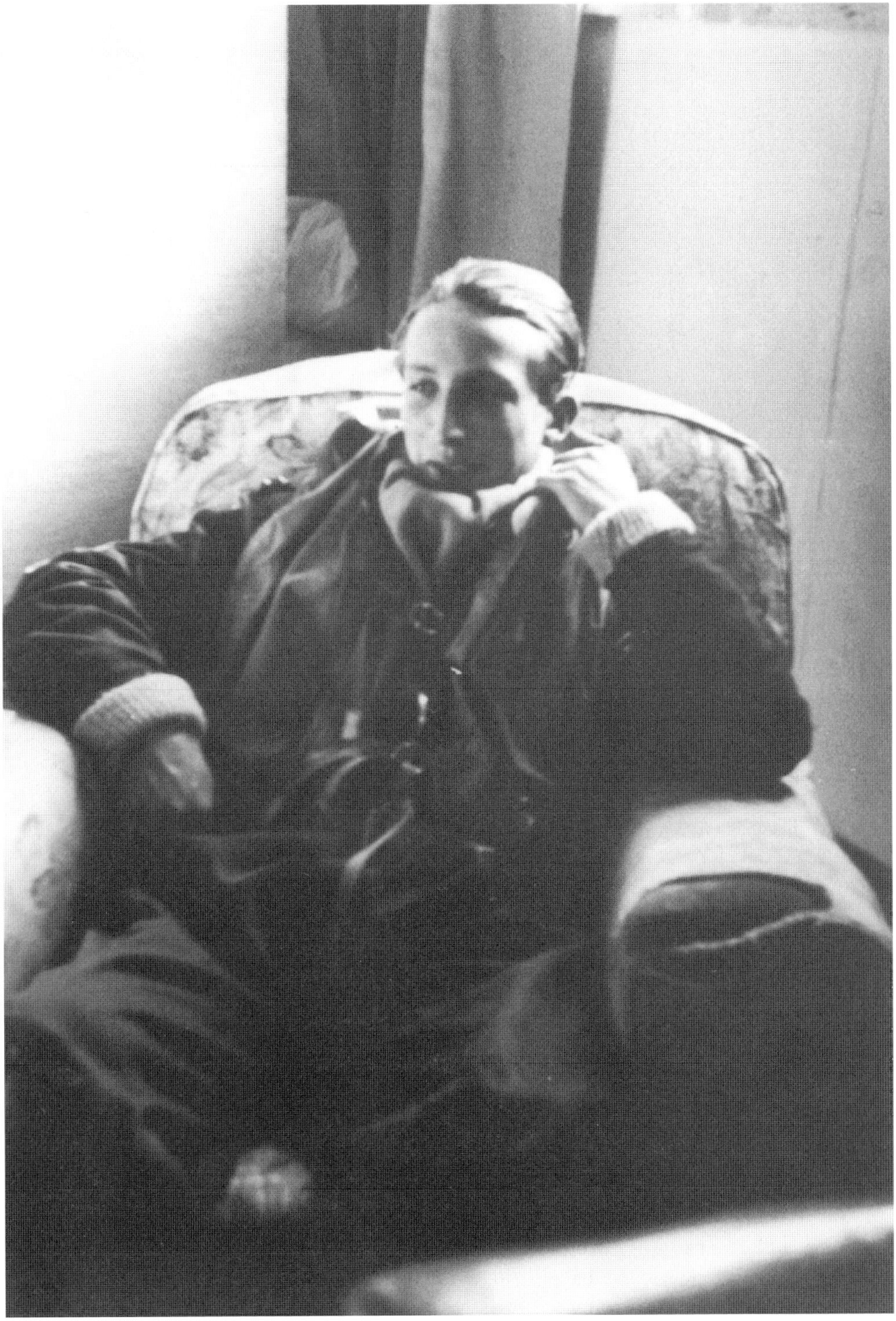

After the Battle of Britain, Peter Brown largely served as a flying instructor, leaving the service as a squadron leader decorated with the Air Force Cross in 1946. Afterwards, he became a major figure in the plastics industry and something of a Battle of Britain historian himself. Squadron Leader Brown is pictured at home in Wilmslow, Cheshire, by the author in 1995, wearing Bielmaier's lifejacket, during the research for *A Few of the Many*, published that year and in which Peter's story was told. He died on 20 January 2011.

Peter Howard-Williams' father was a First World War fighter ace decorated with the Military Cross, and both Peter and his brother, Jeremy, a night-fighter pilot, received Distinguished Flying Crosses in the Second World War. A Cranwellian, Peter flew Spitfires with 19 Squadron at Fowlmere throughout the Battle of Britain before becoming a flight commander on 118 Squadron. Flying from Ibsley, Peter participated in many offensive sorties over France, and survived being very badly shot-up by 109s on 2 February 1942. He is pictured here after his DFC award in 1941.

Peter Howard-Williams eventually retired from the RAF as a wing commander in 1958, after which he lived in Spain for many years. A prolific correspondent, his story was told in *A Few of the Many* (1995), but sadly Peter did not live to see the book published: he succumbed to cancer, aged 73, in March 1993. The author revisited Peter's story in *Spitfire Voices* (2010).

The Short Service Commission attracted many adventurous and intrepid young men from the Empire and Commonwealth to volunteer for flying duties with the RAF, including New Zealander Keith Lawrence. Another incredibly modest man, who would only talk, really, about other people's august deeds and when he was himself shot down. Keith actually saw extensive combat throughout the Battle of Britain flying Spitfires with 234 and 603 Squadrons before transferring to the high-altitude reconnaissance 421 Flight. Later, Keith saw more action over Malta and led 124 Squadron dive-bombing V-2 rocket bases in the Netherlands. Decorated with the DFC, he transferred to the RNZAF returning home to England after the war and settling in Exeter, Devon.

Squadron Leader Keith Lawrence DFC was a great supporter and popular guest at the author's various book launches and other events for many years, his story being told for the first time in *A Few of the Many* (1995) and more recently in *The Last of The Few* (2010). Keith, pictured here at a Worcester Guildhall signing in 2000, died on 2 June 2016.

Bob Poulton was a pre-war volunteer reservist who flew Spitfires towards the end of the Battle of Britain with 616 and 64 Squadrons, both of which were based in 12 Group at the time and with which he saw no action. Posted to 74 'Tiger' Squadron at Biggin Hill in November 1940, Pilot Officer Poulton saw action under the guidance of the legendary Squadron Leader A.G. 'Sailor' Malan, destroying several 109s in 1941. Reported for unauthorised low-flying, Bob was posted away from 74 in August 1941, becoming an instructor. Having survived a mid-air collision with another instructor – also one of The Few, namely Flight Lieutenant John Pickering, who was killed – Bob returned to operational flying as a flight commander on 611 Squadron, destroying a Fw 190 and being awarded the DFC in 1943. The following year his Spitfire developed engine trouble, forcing him to bale out over France, breaking a leg in a heavy landing before being captured. After the war, Bob re-joined the RAF in 1951 as a controller, eventually retiring in 1968.

Flight Lieutenant Bob Poulton DFC is pictured here by the author at his home in Liskeard, Cornwall, in 1995. That year his story was told, in his own words, in *A Few of The Many*, but Bob died in May 1998. His story was revisited more recently in *Spitfire Voices* (2010).

Basil 'Mike' Bush was another reservist mobilised when war broke out, and joined 504 Squadron, flying Hurricanes, just as the Battle of Britain began. On 7 September 1940, operating from Hendon, Sergeant Bush was shot-up and force-landed near Eastchurch, a 20mm cannon shell having ruptured his petrol tank, which leaked fuel into his cockpit – he was lucky not to catch fire. He destroyed a Me 110 and damaged a He 111 before the Squadron was then moved to Filton, near Bristol, in response to German air attacks on West Country aircraft factories. On 30 September 1940 he was amongst 10 Group pilots intercepting a heavy raid which virtually destroyed Sherborne town centre, but forced-landed having run out of fuel. After the Battle of Britain, Mike joined Force Benedict, the RAF deployment flying Hurricanes in Russia, before later serving as an instructor before transferring to Bomber Command and flying Mosquito Pathfinders – for which work he received the DFC. He survived the war and left the service as a flight lieutenant in 1945.

Mike Bush became a bank manager after the war and is pictured here by the author at home in Dunstan, Lincolnshire, in 1994, during his research for *Angriff Westland*. Mike died in 2002.

Yet another pre-war reservist was Ron Stillwell, who converted to Spitfires at Aston Down in July 1940. There he flew Spitfire R6644, which the author and friends recovered from its crash-site near Malvern, Worcestershire, in 1987. During the Battle of Britain, Sergeant Stillwell flew Spitfires with 65 Squadron at Hornchurch, the following year destroying a Me 109 and a Ju 88. In 1942 he was awarded the DFM for his efforts, sadly unsuccessful, to save a ditched pilot in the North Sea. After a spell on Lightnings, Ron, having been commissioned, returned to 65 Squadron as a flight commander, increasing his score further still, and ultimately commanded 122 Squadron. Awarded the DFC, Ron left the service as a squadron leader in 1947. He is pictured here with his 65 Squadron Spitfire Mk IX in 1943.

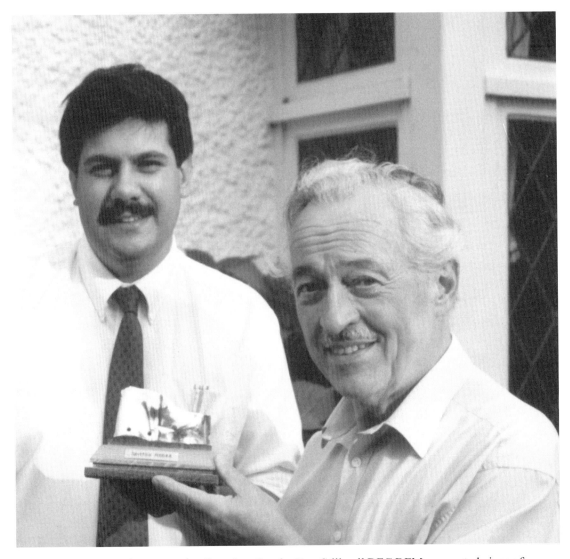

Above: The author presenting Squadron Leader Ron Stillwell DFC DFM a mounted piece of Spitfire R6644, which he flew during training in 1940. The photograph was taken at Ron's home in Hillingdon, Middlesex, in August 1992. Sadly, Ron died the following February, aged 73.

Opposite: Another pilot to fly Spitfire R6644 at Aston Down was David Scott-Malden, who became a most distinguished and highly decorated fighter ace and wing leader, eventually retiring from the service in 1966 as an air vice-marshal.

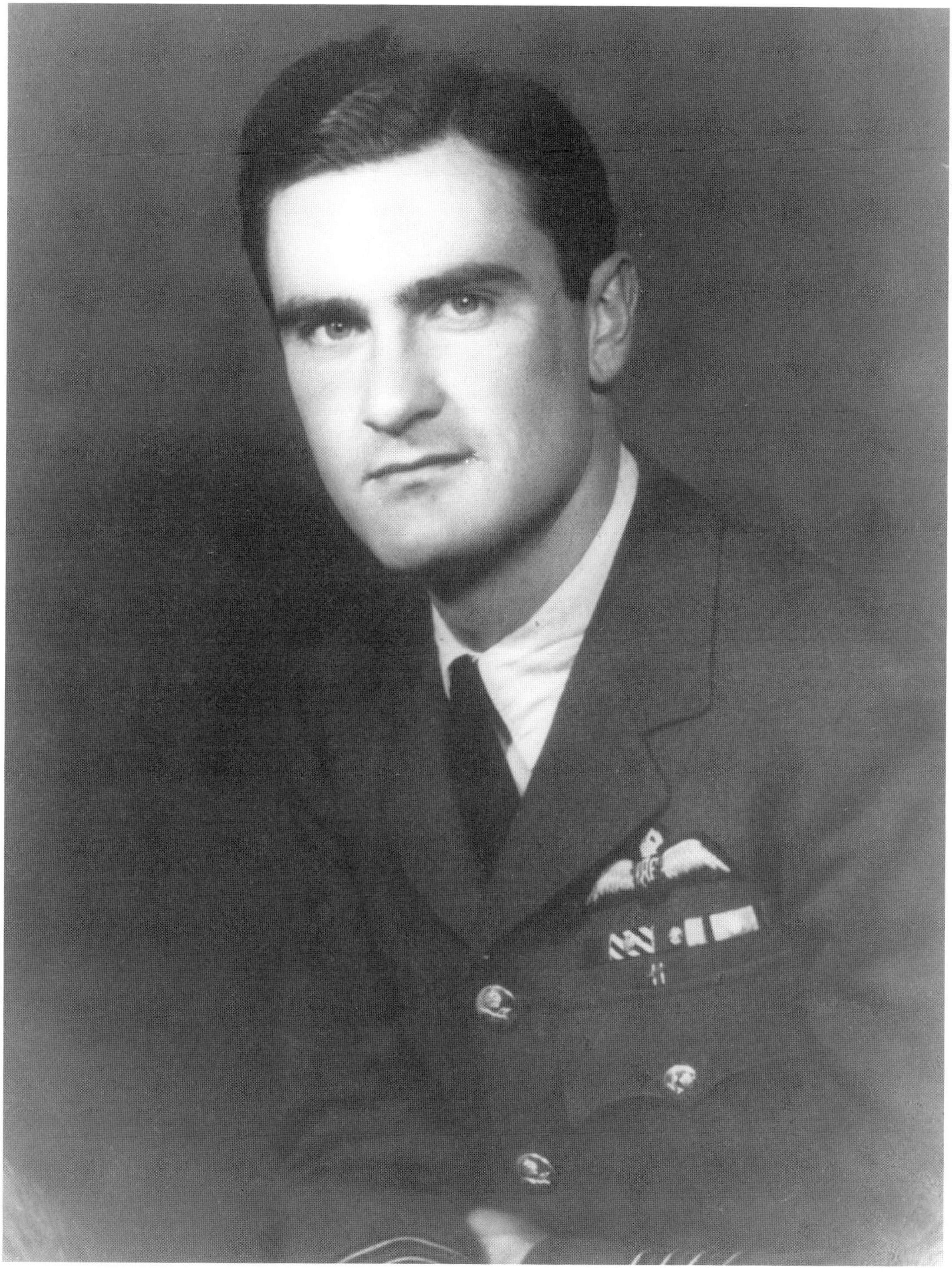

Above: Air Vice-Marshal Scott-Malden was also presented with a mounted item from R6644 by the author in 1992, this photograph being taken at David's Poringland, Norfolk, home; he died on 1 March 2000.

Left: Peter Brothers took a Short Service Commission in 1936, having already learned to fly when aged 16. By May 1940 he was a flight lieutenant commanding a flight of 32 Squadron, flying Hurricanes, and saw much action in the Battle of France and opening stage of the Battle of Britain. With nine enemy aircraft destroyed to his credit, he joined Squadron Leader Bob Stanford-Tuck's 257 Squadron at North Weald, increasing his score further still and receiving the DFC. Peter went on to also become a highly decorated ace and wing leader, surviving the war to become a CBE, participate in Winston Churchill's funeral, and eventually retire as an air commodore in 1973. He is pictured here at Hawkinge during the Battle of Britain.

Air Commodore Peter Brothers was a truly gregarious and enthusiastic character, and another great friend of the author's. Peter is pictured here at Worcester Guildhall signing during the launch of the author's *Battle of Britain: The Photographic Kaleidoscope, Volume III*, to which he contributed the foreword and at which time Peter was Deputy Chairman of the Battle of Britain Fighter Association. Also pictured are the composer Ron Goodwin, armourer Fred Roberts, Flight Lieutenant Richard Jones, (see photograph 7), He 111 pilot Paul Moeller, and another of The Few, Flight Lieutenant Geoffrey Stevens (see photograph 53). Peter died on 18 December 2008.

Left: An early correspondent of the author's was Flight Lieutenant Harry Welford, an auxiliary airman serving with 607 'County of Durham' Squadron during the Battle of Britain. On 15 August 1940, Pilot Officer Welford participated in the so-called 'Junkers Party', when the Germans made a heavy attack on north-eastern England from bases in Norway, during which he destroyed a He 111 and damaged another. The following month he survived being shot down over Kent by Hauptmann Edu Neumann of I/JG 27, and force-landed, wounded. He later served as an instructor before returning to operational flying on Spitfire Mk IXs and Hawker Tempests with the 2nd Tactical Air Force in Europe.

Opposite: Harry Welford, who settled in Sidmouth, Devon, pictured at the launch of the author's *The Invisible Thread: A Spitfire's Tale* at Great Malvern in 1992; he died in 1996, and most recently his story was told in *Letters From The Few: Unique Memories of the Battle of Britain* (2020).

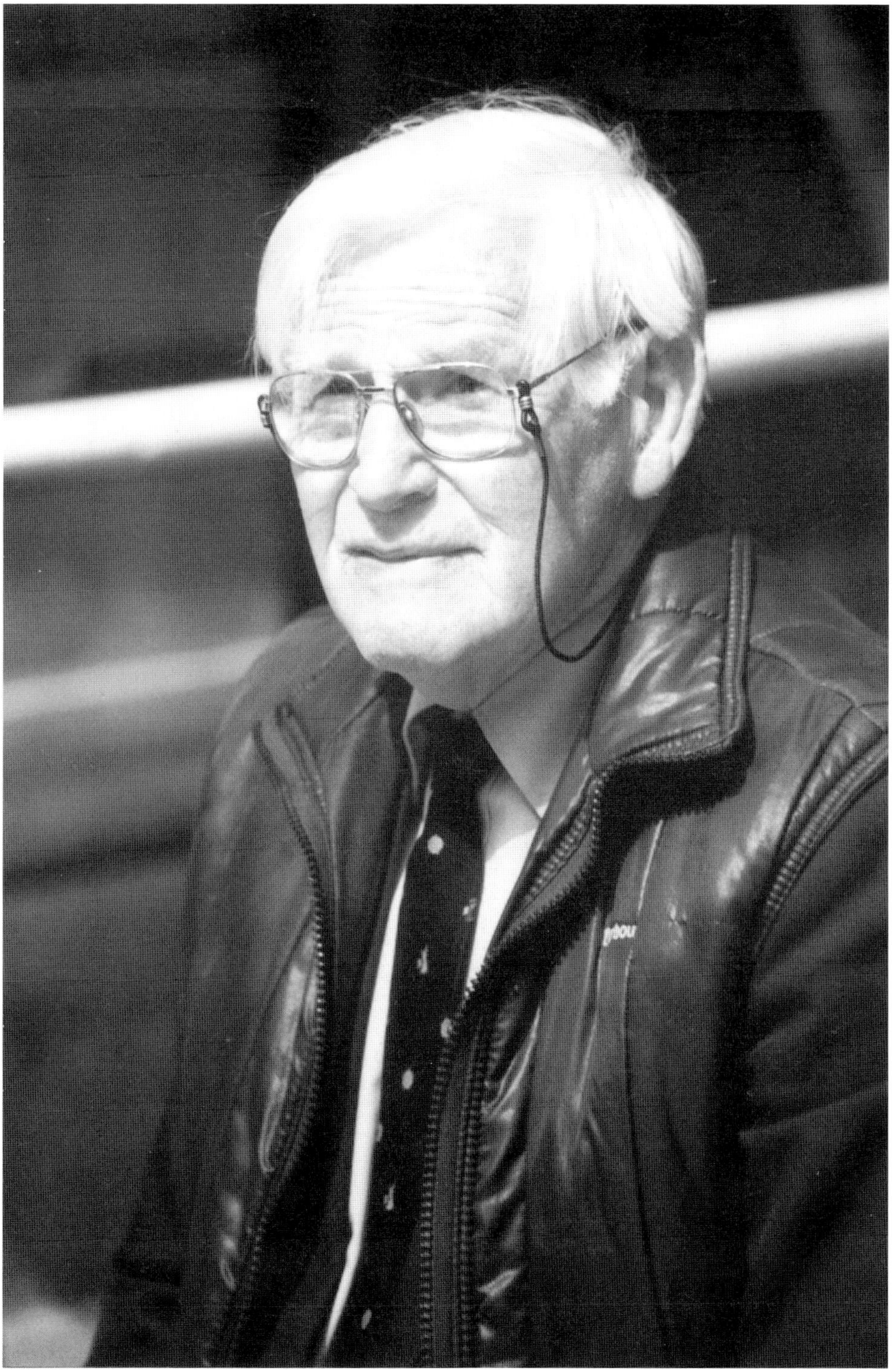

Another, more senior, pilot on 607 Squadron during the Battle of Britain was Flight Lieutenant William Francis Blackadder DSO (fourth from right), pictured here at Tangmere in September 1940 with his 'A' Flight. From left: Sergeant Anderson and Flight Sergeant Atkin (armourers); Sergeant Richard Spyer (killed defending Malta, 22 March 1941); Sergeant William Cunnington (also killed in the defence of Malta, 17 November 1940); Sergeant Fort (Engine Fitter), and A.C. Ventham (rigger). To the Flight Commander's left is Flying Officer Maurice Irving (shot down and killed over the Channel, 28 September 1940); Pilot Officer Watson (Intelligence Officer), and Pilot Officer Michael Ingle-Finch (died 1 February 1942).

Francis (as he was known) Blackadder also became an ace, survived the war, but died in November 1997. Squadron Leader Blackadder DSO OBE is pictured here on 14 November 1993 at Durham Cathedral with another ace, Wing Commander Joe Kayll DSO DFC OBE DL, who fought in the Battle of France with 607 Squadron before commanding 615 Squadron at Kenley during the Battle of Britain. In June 1941, Kayll became Wing Leader at Hornchurch but was shot down over France and captured the following month; he died in March 2000. At right is Flight Lieutenant Harry Welford (see photographs 45 and 46).

Christopher 'Bunny' Currant was a regular pre-war airman fortunate enough to become a fighter pilot under the auspices of the 1936 Expansion Plan, who was, in due course commissioned. Flying Hurricanes with 605 Squadron, he saw extensive combat during the Fall of France and Battle of Britain, becoming an ace decorated with the DFC and Bar. After a rest instructing, Bunny commanded 501 Squadron at Ibsley in 1941, where he appeared amongst other actual operational fighter pilots in the opening scenes of Leslie Howard's film *The First of The Few*, about the Spitfire's designer, R.J. Mitchell. In 1942 he commanded the Ibsley Wing and later 122 Wing of the 2nd TAF. With a final tally of ten enemy aircraft destroyed and another five shared, with two probables and twelve damaged, there is no doubt that Bunny was an exceptional fighter pilot. He remained in the RAF until retiring as a wing commander in 1959, and is pictured here whilst commanding 501 Squadron – note the squadron leader's pennant motif.

Wing Commander Currant DSO DFC* was another popular guest at the author's many events. Badly affected by his wartime experiences, Bunny wrote poems as a means of therapy, some of which are published in the author's *Letters From The Few* (2020). Having settled in Trull, Somerset, Bunny died on 12 March 2006.

Iain Hutchinson was a Glaswegian pre-war volunteer reservist posted to the newly formed 222 Squadron, operating Blenheims, at Duxford in February 1940. In March, the unit converted to Spitfires and moved to Hornchurch two months later, from where it participated in Operation DYNAMO. On 30 August 1940, Sergeant Hutchinson's Spitfire was damaged in combat, but he learned fast, destroying or damaging a number of enemy aircraft over the next few days. On 14 September 1940 he was again shot-up and forced to make an emergency landing, and four days later was shot down by 109s over Canterbury. Baling out slightly wounded, Iain was soon back in action but was shot-up again, on 30 September 1940, and once more force-landed, wounded. After the Battle of Britain, he became a photographic reconnaissance pilot until brought down and captured. This snapshot was taken at Hornchurch during the Battle of Britain – the 'saint' motif appears to have been a popular Mae West adornment.

After retiring from the RAF as a squadron leader in 1957, Iain Hutchinson worked in the energy business and eventually settled in Dorchester, Dorset. He is pictured here at the launch of the author's *The Invisible Thread* at Great Malvern in 1992, and in 1994 joined the author's team for the excavation of Sergeant Denis Nichols' Hurricane at Alton Pancras, Dorset, at which 'Nick' was also present. Squadron Leader Hutchinson died on 27 April 2007.

Geoffrey Stevens was yet another pre-war reservist who, after service flying training, briefly joined 151 Squadron before reporting to 213 Squadron at Tangmere on 14 September 1940. Having damaged an Me 110 on 30 September 1940, on 17 October 1940 Sergeant Stevens was shot down in combat with Me 109s over Ashford, possibly by Gefreiter Karl Raisinger of 3/JG 77, and force-landed, wounded. After recovering, he was later commissioned and served in the Middle East, leaving the service in 1945 but re-joining the following year until 1968. This studio portrait was taken during the Battle of Britain.

Flight Lieutenant Geoffrey Stevens retired to Cheshire and was a stalwart supporter of the author and welcome guest at numerous events over many years; he died on 17 April 2006. His story is told in *Last of The Few* (2010).

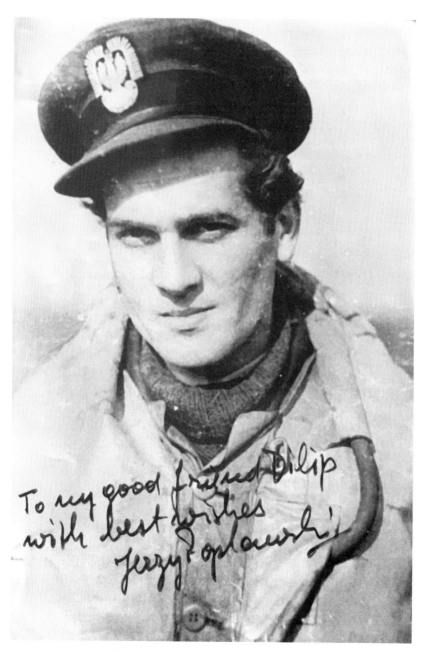

An early correspondent of the author's was Squadron Leader Jurek Poplawski, a Polish pilot who flew Hurricanes during the Battle of Britain with 111 and 229 Squadron, but saw no action at that time. He later became an ace flying Spitfires from Northolt in 1941 with 308 'City of Krakow' Squadron, and ended the war with extensive operational experience, having commanded 315 'City of Deblin' Squadron, decorated with both the Polish Virtuti Militari and Cross of Valour. This photograph was taken at Northolt in 1941.

After the war, Squadron Leader Poplawski emigrated to Buenos Aires, and is pictured here in February 1993 with his Argentinian wife, Maria. He died on 21 June 2004, aged 84.

Flight Lieutenant Ludwik Martel was another Polish pilot embedded in an RAF fighter squadron, and flew Spitfires from Hornchurch during the Battle of Britain with 54 and 603 Squadrons. Pilot Officer Martel damaged an Me 109 on 2 October 1940, and destroyed one three days later. On 25 October 1940 he was flying Spitfire Mk IIA P7350, (still airworthy today and with the Battle of Britain Memorial Flight), when shot-up in combat with Me 109s and wounded, probably by Hauptmann Walter Adolph, Staffelkapitän of 11/JG 26. Ludwik managed to make a wheels-up crash-landing near Hastings, and after recuperating was back in action a few days later. Later in the war he scored further successes in the Middle East, flying with the Polish Fighting Team, better known as 'Skalski's Circus' after their famous commander, the ace Stanislaw Skalski. Eventually leaving the service in 1947, Ludwik settled in Wimbledon, England, and went into business. He remained an active member of the former Polish Air Force Association in Great Britain and the Battle of Britain Fighter Association all his life.

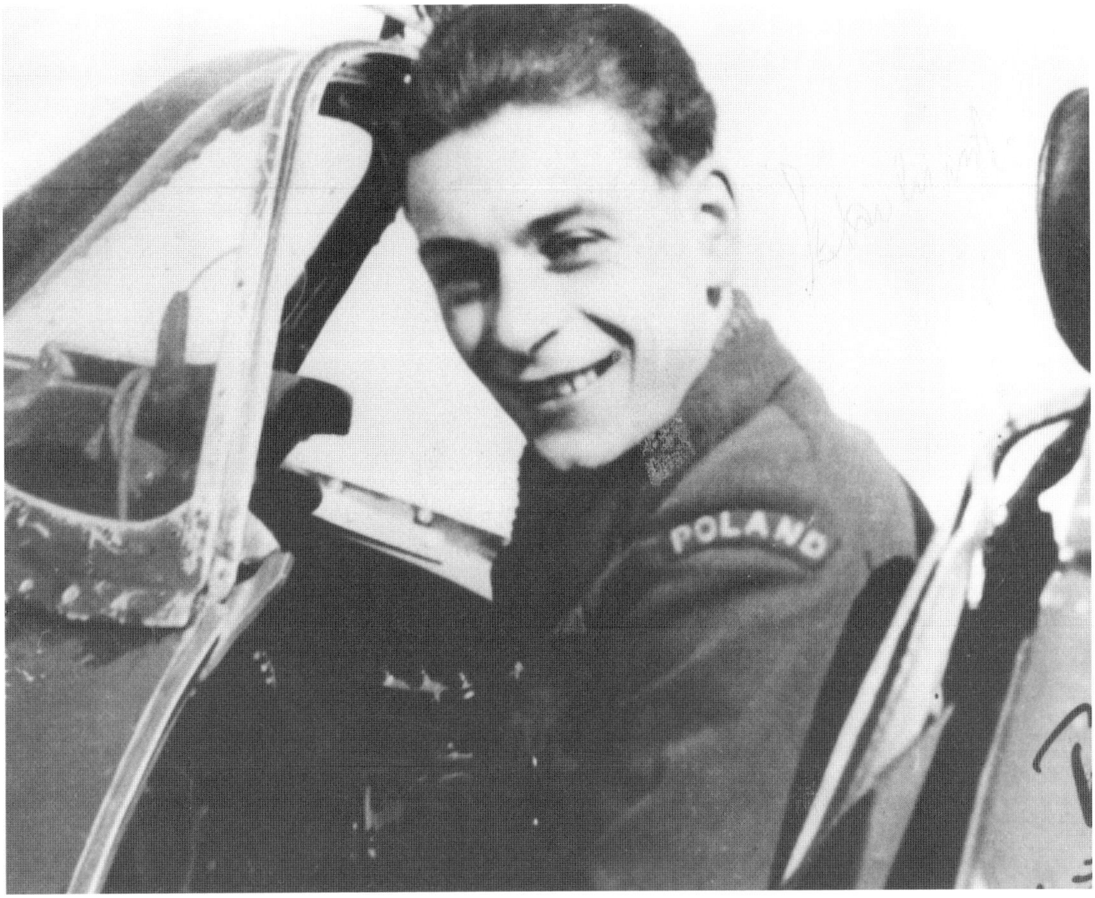
POLAND

Another close Polish friend of the author was Squadron Leader Boleslaw Drobinski DFC, universally known as 'Gandi' on account of his tall and thin build. 'Gandi' also flew in a British squadron during the Battle of Britain, 65, at Hornchurch. Like many others, he became an ace during the bitter fighting of 1941, flying with the famous Polish 303 Squadron at Northolt, a unit he ultimately rose to command in 1944. After the war his application for British citizenship was refused on the grounds that when he landed here in 1940, it was as an illegal immigrant! Disgusted, 'Gandi' consequently lived in America for many years, until eventually returning to England and settling in Dunsfold, Surrey. This photograph was taken at Hornchurch during the Battle of Britain, whilst Pilot Officer Drobinski was serving with 65 Squadron.

Above: On 12 September 1987, Squadron Leader 'Gandi' Drobinski (right) and Flight Lieutenant Ludwik Martel (left) represented the Polish Air Force Association and Battle of Britain Fighter Association when they attended the public recovery of Spitfire R6644 and jointly unveiled the Malvern Spitfire Team's memorial to their fallen comrade, Flying Officer Franek Surma, in Jennet Tree Lane, Madresfield, Worcestershire. The team was led by the author, who, on the say-so of 'Gandi' and Ludwik, was subsequently made an 'honorary Pole' at a special ceremony in London in recognition of the achievement and his pioneering research into Polish fighter pilots. Sadly, 'Gandi' died on 26 July 1995, shortly before which he called the author to say 'goodbye and thank you'. Ludwik died on 25 April 2010, aged 90 – and two finer gentleman could not be imagined.

Opposite: Another reservist was Peter Hutton Fox who, after being called to full-time service and completion of flying training, joined 56 Squadron at Boscombe Down in September 1940. On 30 September 1940, in his first combat, the 19-year-old Hurricane pilot was shot down and baled out over Lyme Regis. The following year he was shot down whilst flying Spitfires with 234 Squadron and captured, as a result of which, much to his displeasure, he was never commissioned, ending the war a warrant officer. In 1994, Peter returned with the author and friends to the crash site of his Hurricane and joined in the excavation. The necessary application for a licence to dig had been made to the Ministry of Defence in Peter's name, and so when ownership of the resulting artefacts recovered was transferred from the Crown to the licence-holder, he became the only one of The Few to actually personally own his Battle of Britain fighter – even if it was in a million pieces!

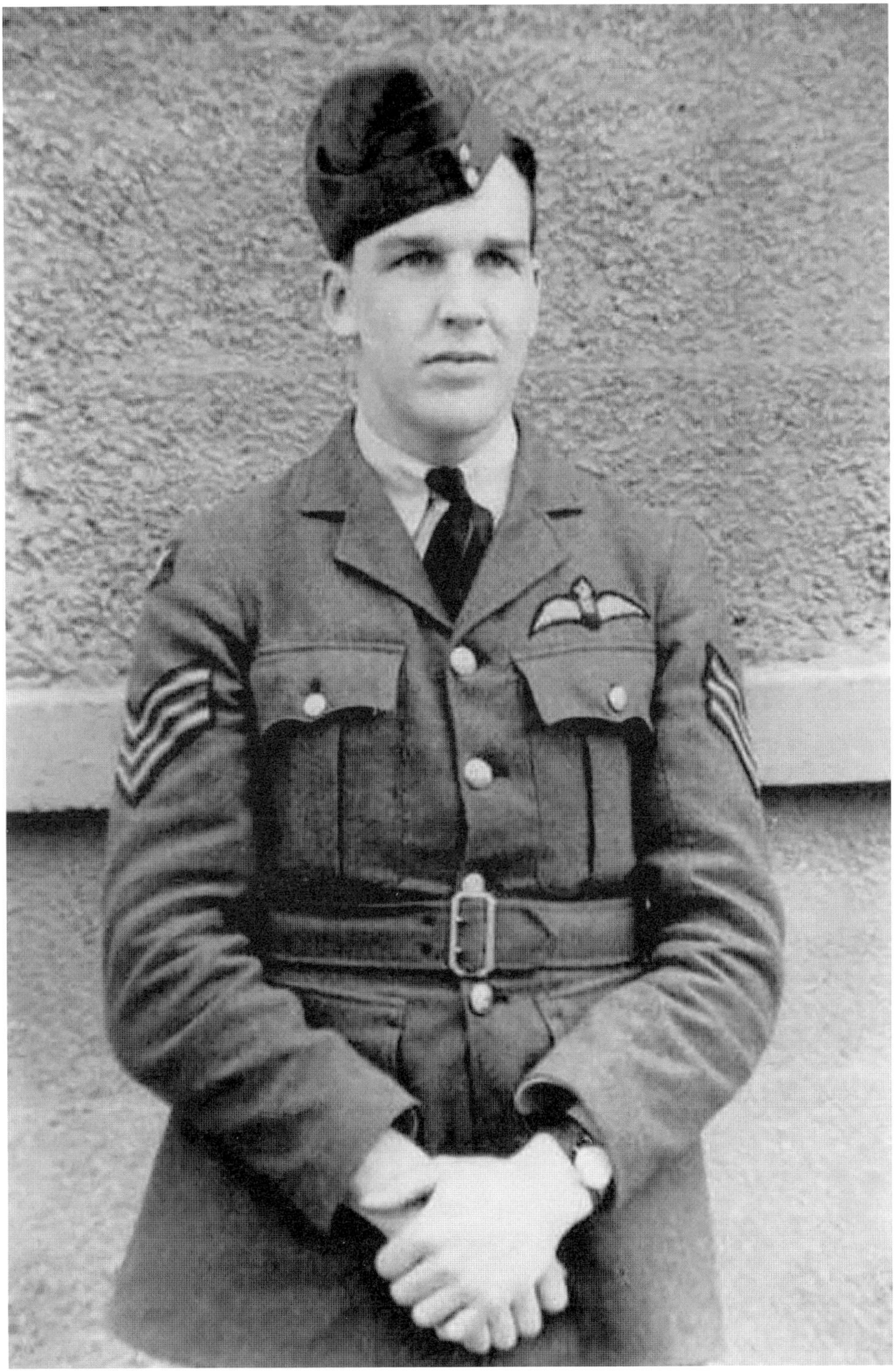

The first of the Few the author actually met, in 1985, was yet another pre-war reservist, namely Tony Garforth Pickering, who, as a sergeant-pilot, had flown Hurricanes throughout much of the Battle of Britain with 501 Squadron, based at Kenley and Gravesend. Tony survived being shot down and baling out over Caterham on 11 September 1940, and got a 109 two days before the Battle ended. After being commissioned and various subsequent postings as an instructor, Tony served in the Middle East. Having left the RAF in 1945, he worked for General Electric and settled in Rugby, Warwickshire, where he was an enthusiastic camponologist.

Also a pre-war reservist, Dennis 'Nick' Nichols trained with his friend Peter Fox and the pair were posted together to 56 Squadron. A week after Peter was shot down, Sergeant Nichols was likewise brought down over Dorset in what was also his first engagement. Baling out, his back was broken in a heavy landing, but fortunately Nick survived to be commissioned and survive the war, during the remainder of which he became a night-fighter pilot, flying Beaufighters in the Middle East. After the war he became a civil airline pilot, and, having retired to Malvern, Worcestershire, like Peter Fox joined the author and team to excavate the crash site of his Hurricane at Alton Pancras, Dorset, in 1994.

Above: Peter Fox (left) became a surveyor after the war, but suffered a personal tragedy when his son, Flight Lieutenant John Hutton Fox, was killed in a flying accident whilst instructing on Jet Provosts on 1 June 1978. Nonetheless, Peter, who retired to Weston-Super-Mare, Avon and Somerset, was an enthusiastic member of the Battle of Britain Fighter Association and attended many of the author's events; he died on 10 June 2005. Squadron Leader Tony Pickering (centre) was likewise a great supporter of Battle of Britain history and events; he died on 24 March 2016. So too was Flight Lieutenant Denis Nichols (right), who left us on 23 August 2001. The trio are pictured at a reunion of The Few hosted by the American Air Force at Alconbury. The author told Tony's story in *A Few of the Many* (1995) and *Last of The Few* (2010), and most recently Peter and 'Nick' were included in *Letters From The Few* (2020).

Opposite: Another reservist, who trained with Peter Fox and Dennis Nichols, and was also a great friend of Tony Pickering's, was Kenneth Anstill Wilkinson, who was posted as a replacement pilot to 19 Squadron at Fowlmere. Ken saw no action in the Battle of Britain, and afterwards served a long spell as an instructor before returning to fly Spitfires operationally with 234 and 165 Squadrons. Ken, a real character and terrific ambassador for The Few post-war, who left the RAF in 1945, shot nothing down, nor was he shot down himself, as a result of which he proudly described his war as 'a no-score draw'! He is pictured here at Ibsley whilst with 165 Squadron in 1943.

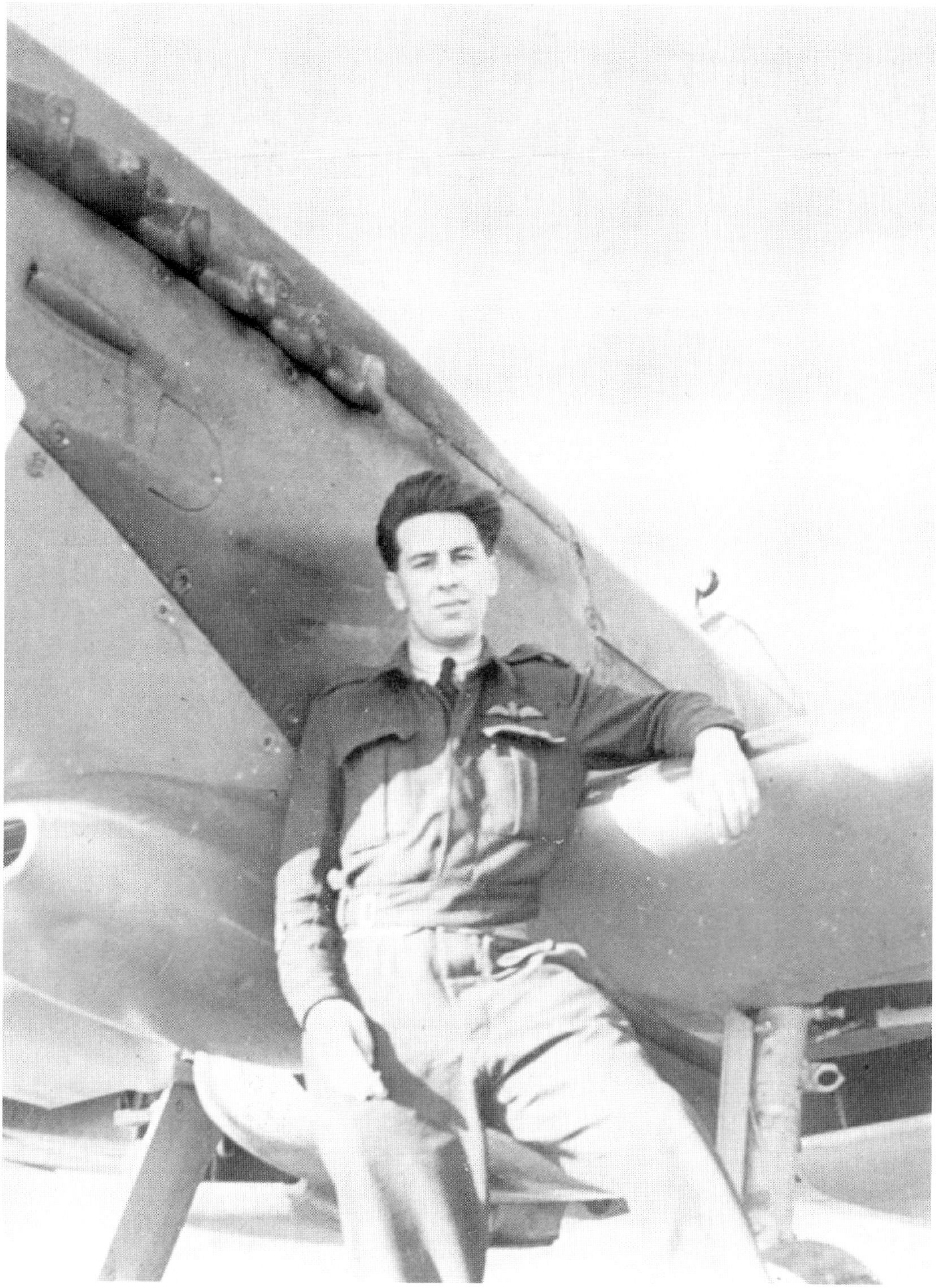

Above: Like Peter Fox, Ken Wilkinson became a surveyor after the war, settling in Solihull, West Midlands. A passionate golfer, incorrigible raconteur and comedian, Flight Lieutenant Wilkinson is pictured here wearing his original Irvin flying jacket and showing his flying boots. Ken died on 31 July 2017, and the author, having spent many hours with him since their first meeting in 1988, was honoured to speak at his funeral. Ken's story is told in full, in his own words, in *The Final Few* (2015).

Opposite: The Battle of Britain, however, was not just fought by Hurricane and Spitfire pilots. This is the Canadian Flight Lieutenant George Pushman, who flew twin-engine Bristol Blenheims with 23 Squadron throughout the Battle of Britain, mainly at night. Later, whilst flying Bostons with 88 Squadron, he was awarded the DFC for his bravery laying down a smoke screen on the D-Day invasion beaches. The photograph was taken in front of his Boston in 1944.

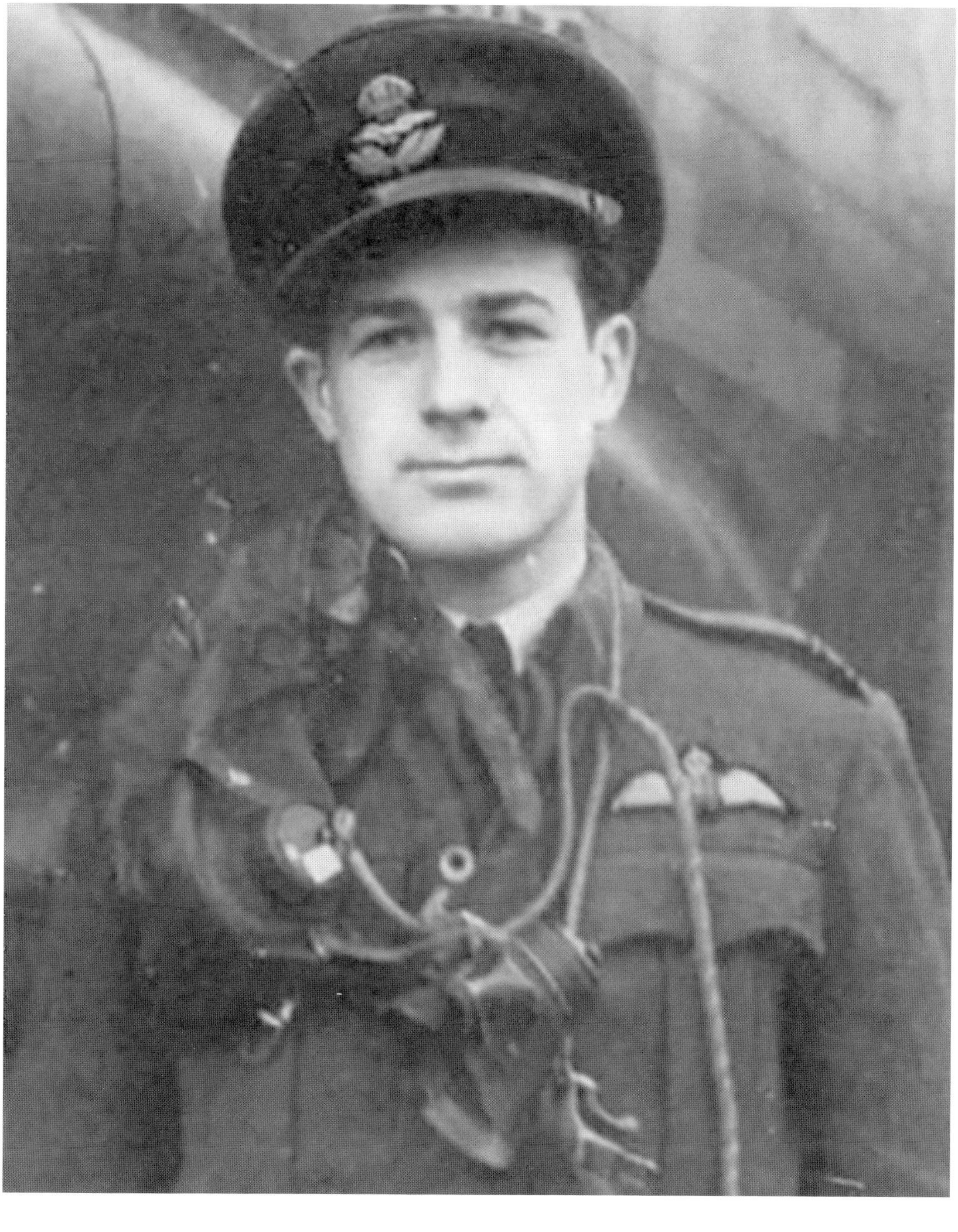

Above: In 1943, Flight Lieutenant Pushman married a WAAF officer, Muriel Gane, the couple eventually retiring to Madresfield, Worcestershire. Muriel became an author, publishing several books, including her wartime memoir, *We All Wore Blue*. The couple are pictured with the author at Worcester Guildhall in 2000. Sadly, George died on 11 April 2011, and Muriel has likewise since departed.

Opposite: Pilot Officer William Walker was also a pre-war reservist. Posted to 616 Squadron at Leconfield to fly Spitfires in June 1940, having survived a nocturnal crash during training at Brize Norton, he went to Kenley with the Squadron on 19 August 1940. Almost immediately the Squadron was embroiled in combat. On 26 August 1940, William's section was bounced whilst climbing over Dover, and he was amongst the pilots shot down. Baling out with an enemy bullet in his ankle, he was fortunately rescued by a passing ship. Upon recovery, his return to operations in May 1941 was brief, and he saw the remainder of the war out as an instructor. During the traumatic fifteen days 616 had spent at Kenley in August and September 1940, 616 Squadron lost eleven Spitfires destroyed and three damaged, with five pilots killed, one wounded and another captured.

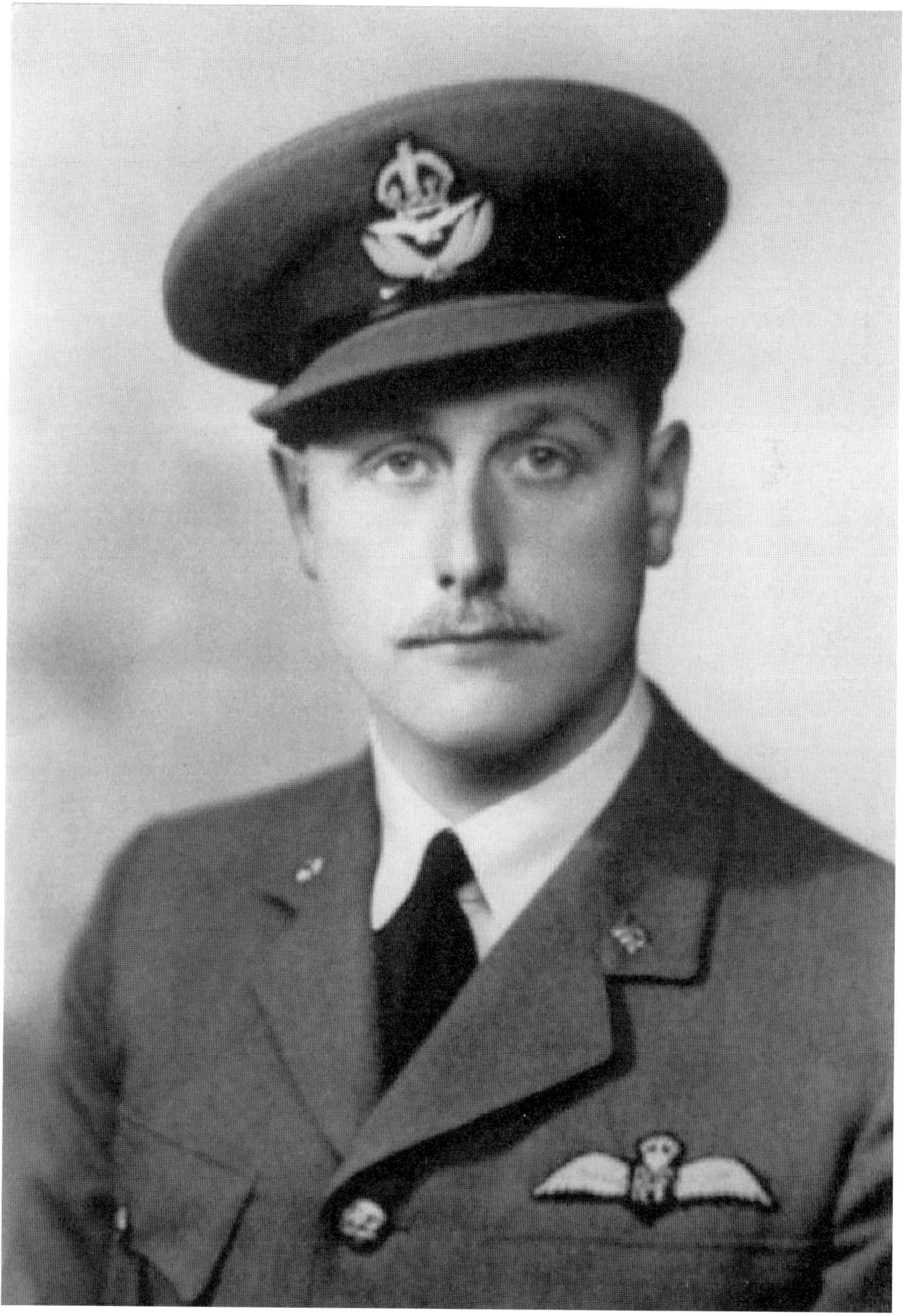

Above: Retiring from the RAF as a flight lieutenant, William Walker became Chairman of a brewery and retired to London. For many years he attended the author's events and was a great supporter of the Battle of Britain Fighter Association and Memorial Trust. The author ascertained that on 26 August 1940, William was most likely shot down by none other than Major Werner Mölders himself, the so-called 'Father of Modern Air Fighting'. Upon receiving this news, William's reaction was 'Well, may as well have been by the top man!' William always carried the bullet removed from his ankle as a talisman, and is pictured here with the author and said round at Worcester Guildhall in 2000. He died on 21 October 2012, aged 99. William's story is told, in his own words, in *Letters From The Few* (2020).

Opposite: Another early supporter was Squadron Leader Lionel 'Buck' Casson AFC DFC, who also survived 616 Squadron's traumatic time at Kenley during the summer of 1940. Buck became an experienced and successful fighter pilot and a prominent member of Wing Commander Douglas Bader's famous Tangmere Wing during the summer of 1941. Shot down by Oberleutnant Gerhard Schöpfel of III/JG 26 over the Pas-de-Calais on the same day as Bader, 9 August 1941, Buck became a prisoner. After the war he commanded 616 Squadron, flying Gloster Meteor jets and retired to his native Sheffield. The author has told his story, in full, several times, the latest of which is contained in the author's *Spitfire Down*, published by Pen & Sword (2022).

To Dilip
With Best Wishes
from
'Buck' Casson

Group Captain Sir Hugh 'Cocky' Dundas was another great friend and 616 Squadron supporter, who survived being shot down in the Battle of Britain and went on to become one of Wing Commander Bader's right-hand men at Tangmere, and one of the service's youngest group captains. A decorated ace, his brother John was shot down and reported missing in action with 109s over the Solent on 28 November 1940. After the war, Sir Hugh became Chairman of Rediffusion and was heavily involved in both the Imperial War Museum (IWM) and RAF Benevolent Fund. His wartime memoir, *Flying Start* remains a classic.

Former members of 616 Squadron outside Buckingham Palace during the 50th anniversary commemorations in September 1990. At second left, standing, is Group Captain Sir Hugh Dundas (died 1995), and to his left is Group Captain Denys 'Kill 'em' Gillam DSO** DFC (died 1991). Second from right is Squadron Leader Buck Casson (died 2003).

Roger Boulding took a Short Service Commission in 1938, and by October 1939 was in France, flying Fairey Battles with 142 Squadron. Back in England after France fell, Roger converted to Spitfires and joined Sailor Malan's 74 Squadron. He soon opened his account as a fighter pilot and was an excellent pilot, there being no better demonstration of his skill than on the night of 10/11 May 1941, when he destroyed a He 111 after a low-level chase across Kent. On a sweep over France on 17 June 1941, Roger was shot down and captured, spending the rest of the war as a prisoner. Permanently commissioned into the peacetime air force, he enjoyed a long career, during which he commanded 249 Squadron on Vampires in Egypt, and became Station Commander of RAF Coningsby. Wing Commander Boulding left the RAF in 1966 and became a hotelier, eventually retiring to Chard, Somerset. The young Pilot Officer Boulding is pictured here shortly after receiving his 'wings'.

In retirement Wing Commander Boulding became a great friend and supporter, and is pictured here (left) with Polish Spitfire pilot Kazek Budzik at the opening of the Malvern Spitfire Team's exhibition at Tudor House Museum, Worcester, in 1988. Roger died on 2 March 1993.

Above: David Cox was yet another reservist and sergeant-pilot, who flew Spitfires with 19 Squadron throughout the Battle of Britain, during which he survived being bombed on the ground at both Eastchurch and Fowlmere, and being shot down. He became an ace, decorated with the DFC and Bar, and also saw combat over North Africa and served in Burma. On 15 September 1980, the Battle of Britain's 40th anniversary, this former commander of 1 Squadron was flown over London in a Lightning jet interceptor. Wing Commander Cox was a prolific correspondent in retirement, living in Lower Earley, Reading, and heavily contributed his experiences to the author's *Spitfire! The Full Story of a Unique Battle of Britain Fighter Squadron* (2019).

Left: Wing Commander Cox pictured at home by the author in 1990; David died on 20 January 2004.

Dennis Adams was initially a volunteer reservist who was commissioned into the Auxiliary Air Force, joining 611 Squadron in July 1938. Over Dunkirk in June 1940 he destroyed a Ju 87 and probably destroyed a 109, and on 21 September 1940 destroyed a Do 215 reconnaissance bomber over North Wales. At the end of that month he was transferred to 41 Squadron, and was shot down, baling out safely, on 7 October 1940. He is pictured here at Tern Hill in Shropshire, in an early Spitfire Mk I.

Squadron Leader Dennis Adams retired to South Africa after, in his words, 'a somewhat mediocre war', and went into business. Quite a character, he was an avid angler and another prolific correspondent. Sadly, by 1992 he was suffering from Alzheimer's, and died on 20 November 1995. His story is included in *Letters From The Few* (2020).

Basil 'Stapme' Stapleton DFC was a South African flying officer with 603 Squadron during the Battle of Britain and another ace. In 1993, the author's research confirmed that on 5 September 1940, Stapleton had shot down the Me 109 of Stab II/JG 3's Oberleutnant Franz von Werra, later infamous as the only German prisoner to escape Allied custody during the Second World War – immortalised by Hardy Kruger in the film *The One That Got Away*.

Stapleton survived the war, during which he also flew Typhoons operationally, and was another enthusiastic attender of Battle of Britain events until his death on 13 April 2010.

Bob Beardsley was a volunteer reservist and sergeant-pilot flying Spitfires with 41 and 610 Squadrons during the Battle of Britain. Having survived being shot-up and crash-landing twice, Bob was commissioned, became an ace, decorated with the DFC, and flew numerous offensive sorties over France in 1941. He is pictured here with his wife, Eileen, outside Buckingham Palace after the DFC investiture in late 1941.

Above: Squadron Leader Bob Beardsley survived the war, during which he also served in the Middle East and on the continent. In 1945 he left the service but re-joined in 1949, flying jets, later becoming a controller. After retiring from the RAF in 1970, Bob became a teacher, and is pictured here with Eileen on the occasion of their 60th wedding anniversary party in July 2000. Bob died on 17 October 2003.

Opposite: Josef Szlagowski was a fighter pilot and flying instructor in Poland before the war, and amongst the first Poles to arrive in England to continue the fight in 1940. After converting to Spitfires, he joined 234 Squadron at St Eval on 4 August 1940, damaging a Do 17 four days later. In September he enjoyed several more combat successes before joining 152 Squadron at Warmwell on 21 October 1940. In March 1941, he joined 303 (Polish) Squadron at Northolt and fought in the Non-Stop Offensive that year. Afterwards, he served as an instructor, leaving the Polish Air Force in 1946.

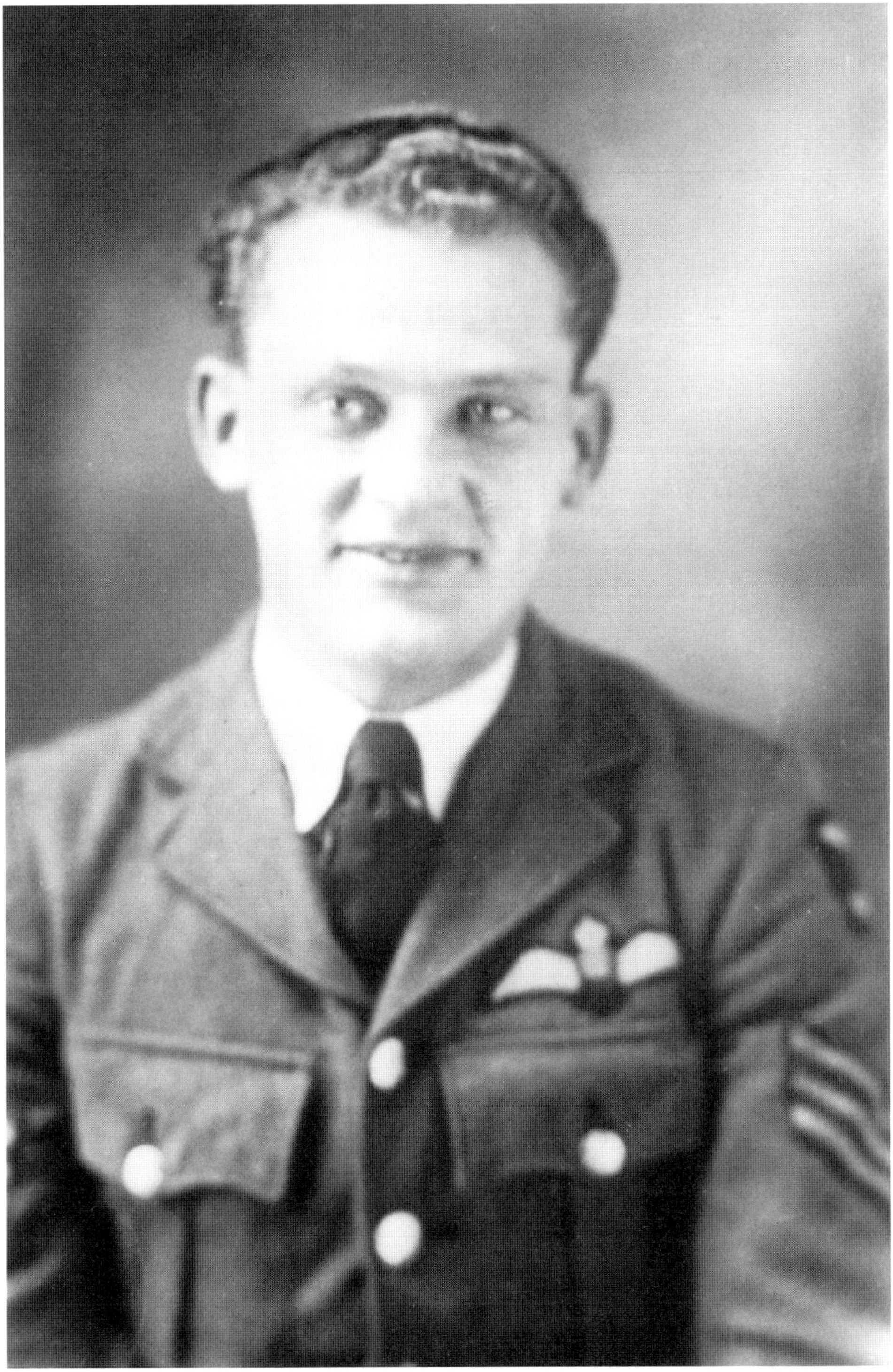

Another Polish pilot was Anton Markiewicz, who first served as an aircraft mechanic in the Polish Air Force, then became an officer pilot in 1936. On 1 September 1939, the day Germany invaded his homeland, Anton destroyed a Hs 126 – which may have been the first German aircraft destroyed in the Second World War. After further victories, including a Do 17 whilst serving with the French, he arrived in England via North Africa and was given the rank of sergeant in the RAFVR. On 6 August 1940 he joined the Polish 302 Squadron, which contributed to Douglas Bader's 'Big Wing' the following month – explaining to the author how 'displeased' Squadron Leader Bader was if the enemy was not encountered. After the Battle of Britain, on 10 February 1941, his Hurricane touched the sea during low-level practice attacks, and Sergeant Markiewicz was seriously injured when he consequently crashed in Sussex. He never flew again operationally and left the service in November 1945.

Both Josef 'Zag' Szlagowski (left) and Anton Markiewicz (right) settled in the UK after the war. Zag worked in the Wilkinson Sword factory and lived in Fulham, and was featured in the excellent 1980 documentary *Churchill's Few*, made by John Willis (see bibliography); he died on 4 December 1993. Anton changed his surname to Martin and became a television engineer, living in South Croydon, and died on 30 April 2005.

Another pilot featured in the inspirational documentary *Churchill's Few* was Wing Commander Bob Doe, who had taken a Short Service Commission in 1938. During the Battle of Britain he became an ace, flying Spitfires with 234 Squadron, awarded the DFC and Bar, before transferring to fly Hurricanes as a flight commander on 238 Squadron. On 10 October 1940, Bob was shot down and baled out, wounded, over Dorset – but worse was to follow after he re-joined 234 Squadron: on 3 January 1941, oil froze in his Spitfire's cooling system, causing him to make an emergency dead stick landing back at a snow covered Warmwell. Upon impact, his Sutton harness broke, and Bob's face was smashed against the reflector gunsight. Following twenty-two operations and facial reconstruction, Bob resumed operational flying and later served in the Far East, receiving the Indian DSO. Remaining in the post-war RAF, he eventually retired in 1966.

Wing Commander Bob Doe retired to Kent and ran a garage. Here, he is pictured being shown the 'office' of a Tornado at RAF Coningsby. Bob died on 21 February 2010.

An informal snapshot of a group of 501 Squadron pilots, from left: Pilot Officers James 'Ginger' Lacey DFM, Ken MacKenzie DFC, Tony Whitehouse, Bob Dafforn and Vic Ekins. All survived the war – but Dafforn was killed on 2 December 1945 whilst serving as a test pilot.

Above: The debonair Peter Townsend, a pre-war Cranwellian pictured whilst serving as a flight commander on 43 Squadron in early 1940, with his Flight Rigger, Duxbury, and Engine Fitter, Hacking. On 3 February 1940, Flight Lieutenant Townsend's Blue Section destroyed the first German aircraft to crash in England since 1918, a KG 26 He 111 that crashed near Whitby. During the Battle of Britain, Peter commanded 85 Squadron and became a highly decorated ace.

Opposite: Squadron Leader 'Ginger' Lacey (left) was one of the highest scoring RAF fighter aces in the Battle of Britain, and later saw action in the Far East; he died on 30 May 1989. Group Captain Peter Townsend (right) became equerry to King George VI and a household name owing to his globally publicised romance with Princess Margaret, recently given currency by the Netflix series *The Crown*. Peter was a great friend of the author's, a philanthropist, journalist and historian whose story is told in *Letters From The Few*; he died in France on 19 June 1995. The pair are pictured here whilst historical consultants working on the 1969 *Battle of Britain* film.

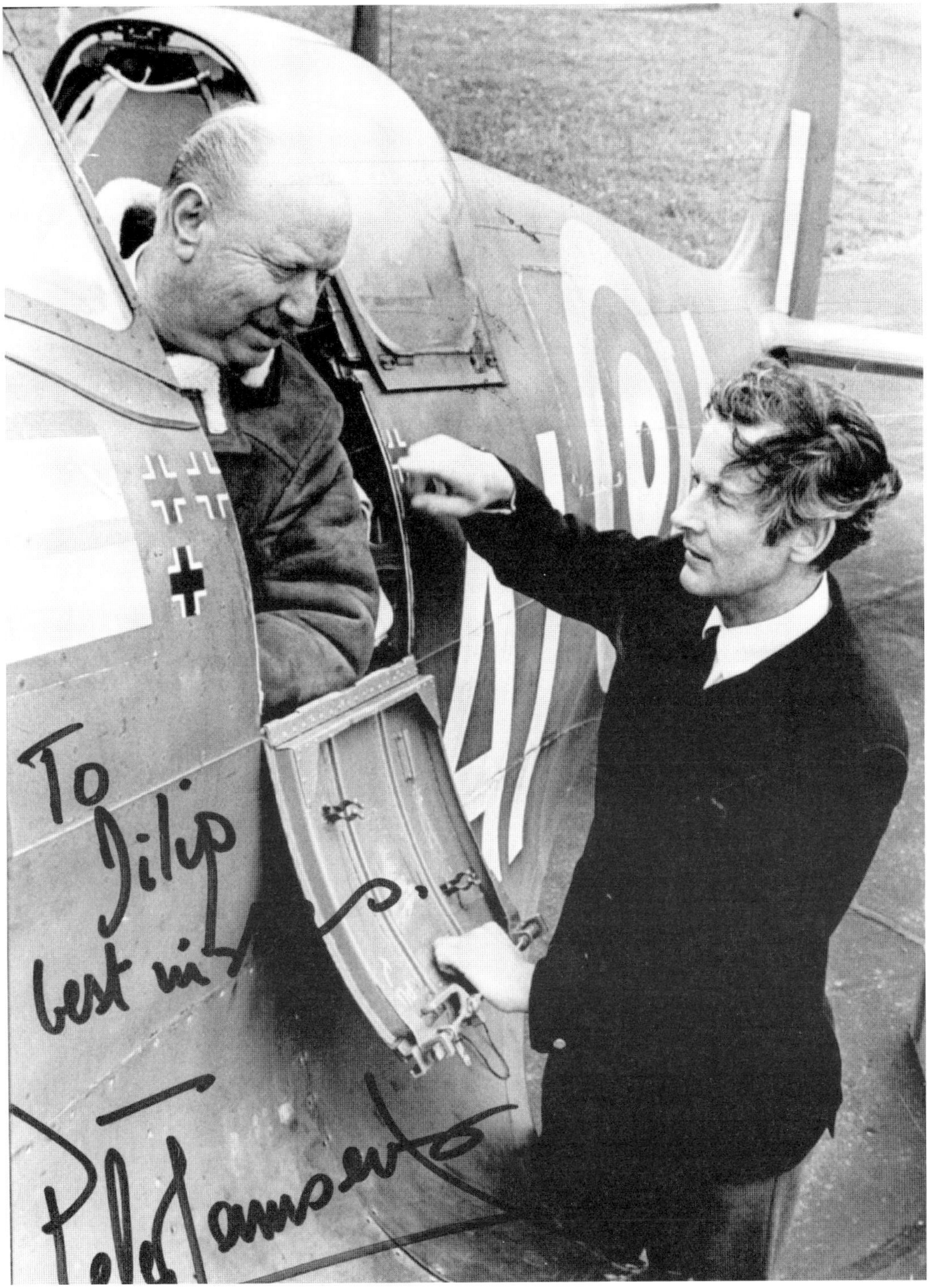
To Dilip

Whilst the Canadian John Kent's association with the famous Polish 303 Squadron is well-known, in no small part owing to his memoir *One of The Few*, the unit's actual British commander's story is less so. This is he, namely Ronald Gustave Kellett, a pre-war stockbroker, Conservative MP-hopeful at the 1931 General Election, and member of the socially elite Auxiliary Air Force. Kellett was a fluent French-speaker and had experience in forming new squadrons, for which reasons he was chosen to raise and command 303 Squadron. Polish officers 'shadowed' their English counterparts, and an excellent working relationship developed thanks to Kellett's sympathetic attitude towards the Poles.

During the Battle of Britain, Squadron Leader Kellett was shot-up badly – but with great skill he managed to land safely at Biggin Hill. He became an ace, receiving the 'double' of DSO and DFC. In the spring of 1941, he was amongst the first wing leaders appointed, going to North Weald and participating in the early operations over France during the Non-Stop Offensive of that year. Later, he was attached to the Turkish Air Force, returning to the Stock Exchange after the war. In 1946, Wing Commander Kellett returned to the AAF, commanding 615 Squadron at Biggin Hill. His story features in the author's *Forgotten Heroes of the Battle of Britain*.

Above: Laurence 'Rubber' Thorogood was a volunteer reservist and sergeant-pilot, posted to fly Hurricanes with 87 Squadron in June 1940. He saw action throughout the Battle of Britain, mainly over the West Country, flying from Exeter and Bibury, this photograph having been taken at the latter. The Hurricane is that of the Squadron Commander, namely Squadron Leader Ian 'Widge' Gleed; all of 87's aircraft were adorned with Disney characters, in this case, Figaro from *Pinocchio*. 'Rubber' was a keen photographer, and some 80 of his photographs appear in the Pen & Sword edition of Gleed's *Arise to Conquer*, introduced and captioned by the author.

Opposite: After several combat successes, 'Rubber' Thorogood was commissioned, later commanded a Spitfire squadron in India, and awarded the DFC; he remained in the RAF until 1964. Having retired to Cambridge, Squadron Leader Thorogood DFC was another welcome guest at book signings and other events organised by the author at IWM Duxford. He died on 30 December 2020.

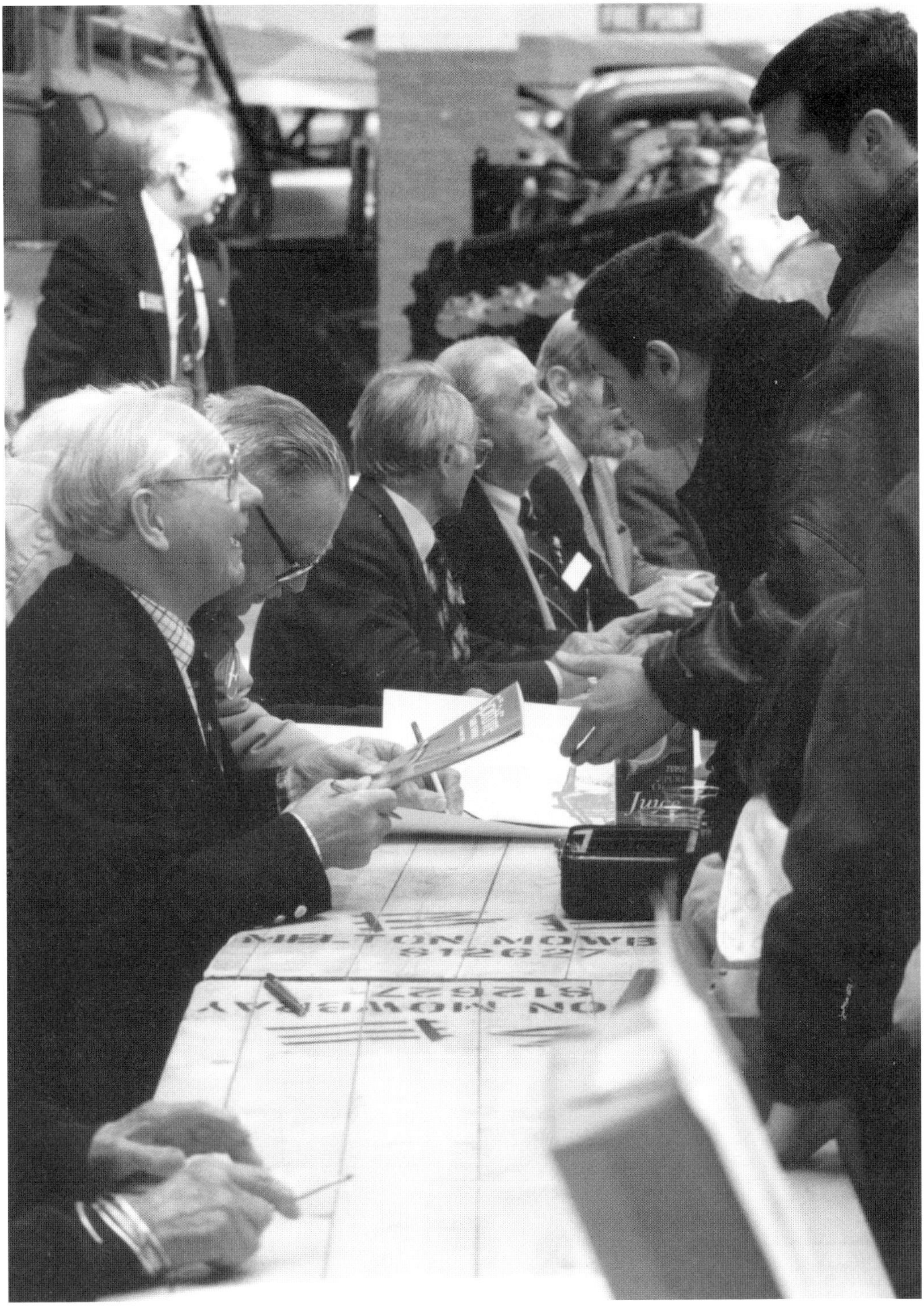
812627
ON MOWBRAY
812627

Above: The surprisingly quiet and shy John Cunningham (right) became one of the RAF's greatest night-fighter pilots, and is pictured here with his radar operator and observer, Jimmy Rawnsley. For security reasons the press attributed his success to exceptional night-vision, assisted by eating carrots, leading to his nickname 'Cat's Eyes' – which John hated!

Opposite left: After leaving the service as a group captain, John Cunningham became a famous post-war test pilot, test-flying, amongst many other things, the De Havilland Comet – the first ever jet airliner. He is pictured here by the author at home in 1990, with the propeller blade from his 13th victory, presented to him at the time, a He 111 destroyed over Cranborne Chase in 1941.

Below: Flying Officer Franek Gruszka was a pre-war pilot and officer in the Polish Air Force, and amongst the first Poles to be trained by the RAF in England and posted to British squadrons during the Battle of Britain. Gruszka was also the first Polish fighter pilot to be killed in action during the summer of 1940, whilst flying Spitfires at Hornchurch with 65 Squadron. On 18 August 1940, he was reported missing after an engagement with Me 109s over Kent – but his aircraft and remains were not recovered until the 1970s. Flying Officer Gruszka was then given a long overdue military funeral at Northwood Cemetery. His story is told in full in the author's *Battle of Britain 1940: The Finest Hour's Human Cost* (2020).

An excellent study of Pilot Officer Desmond Williams of 92 Squadron. Having first seen action over Dunkirk, he became an ace during the Battle of Britain – but was sadly killed in a mid-air collision with another Spitfire whilst attacking a German bomber; Williams was just twenty-years-old.

Another superb snapshot, this of 66 Squadron's Pilot Officer Crelin 'Bogle' Bodie, believed taken at Kenley during the Battle of Britain. Bodie actually flew the first operation of Fighter Command's 1941 offensive on 10 January 1941, a low-level nuisance raid by a pair of Spitfires looking for targets of opportunity over the French coast. An ace decorated with the DFC, he sadly lost his life, aged 21, in a flying accident.

Wing Commander John Scatliffe Dewar DSO DFC was the highest-ranking RAF officer killed during the Battle of Britain. A Cranwellian and highly experienced pre-war officer, 'Johnny' commanded 87 Squadron during the Fall of France and was amongst the first four officers awarded the 'double' of DSO and DFC. During the Battle of Britain he commanded RAF Exeter, continuing to fly operationally with his old Squadron. On 11 September 1940, he was in transit between Exeter and Tangmere when he ran into a large German raid over Southampton. Reported missing, his body was later washed ashore. The author's detailed investigation into this casualty appeared in *The Final Few* (2015), leading to the incorrect date of death on the pilot's headstone at North Baddesley Church being amended.

Another pilot lost in action over the Solent, on 14 August 1940, was Flying Officer Henry MacDonald Goodwin, an auxiliary Spitfire pilot with 609 'West Riding' Squadron, based at Warmwell. 'Mac' was taken home and buried at St Cassian's, Chaddesley Corbett, Worcestershire – joining his brother, Pilot Officer Barrie Goodwin of 605 'County of Warwick' Squadron, who died in a flying accident in June 1940.

Cranwellian Air Commodore Horace 'Tubby' Mermagen was a pre-war aerobatic pilot and flying instructor who formed 222 Squadron on Blenheims at Duxford in October 1939, then converted the unit to Spitfires the following March. He saw action over Dunkirk, receiving the Air Force Cross, but was posted away at the end of July 1940. Thereafter he served in numerous roles, at home and abroad, remaining in the RAF until retiring to Painswick, Gloucestershire, in 1960. 'Tubby', a keen golfer, died in 1998, and his story is told in the author's *Letters From The Few* (2020).

Above: Amongst Mermagen's pilots in 222 Squadron at the time of Dunkirk was the legless, indomitable, Flight Lieutenant Douglas Bader – pictured here with pipe at Manston during Operation DYNAMO. At left is Sergeant Joseph Inkerman Johnson, who would be killed during the Battle of Britain; wearing sunglasses is Pilot Officer Eric Edsall, later killed fighting against the Japanese, and at right is Flying Officer Hilary Edridge, also subsequently killed during the Battle of Britain. Bader became a prisoner of war in 1941, and survived the war to become a household name owing to Paul Brickhill's globally best-selling biography *Reach for the Sky*, and Daniel Angel's film of the same name starring Kenneth More (David Bickers, Douglas Bader Foundation).

Opposite above: Another snapshot taken at Manston during DYNAMO: from left, Flying Officer Hilary Edridge (222 Squadron); unknown; Flight Lieutenants Douglas Bader (222) and Robert Stanford Tuck (92 Squadron), and Flying Officer Bob 'Dutch' Holland (92). Like Bader, Tuck became an ace, a wing leader and prisoner who survived the war. Holland also survived – only to be killed flying Vampire jet fighters in 1954.

Opposite below: Free Czechs also fought in the Battle of Britain, and 310 (Czech) Squadron, based at Duxford on Hurricanes, also operated a 'double-banking' system of Czech officers shadowing British counterparts. These 310 Squadron three pilots are all British; from left: the mercurial Flying Officer Michael Boulton; Flight Lieutenants Jerrard Jeffries and Gordon Sinclair. On 9 September, Boulton and Sinclair collided whilst in combat with Me 110s – Boulton was killed whilst Sinclair safely baled out.

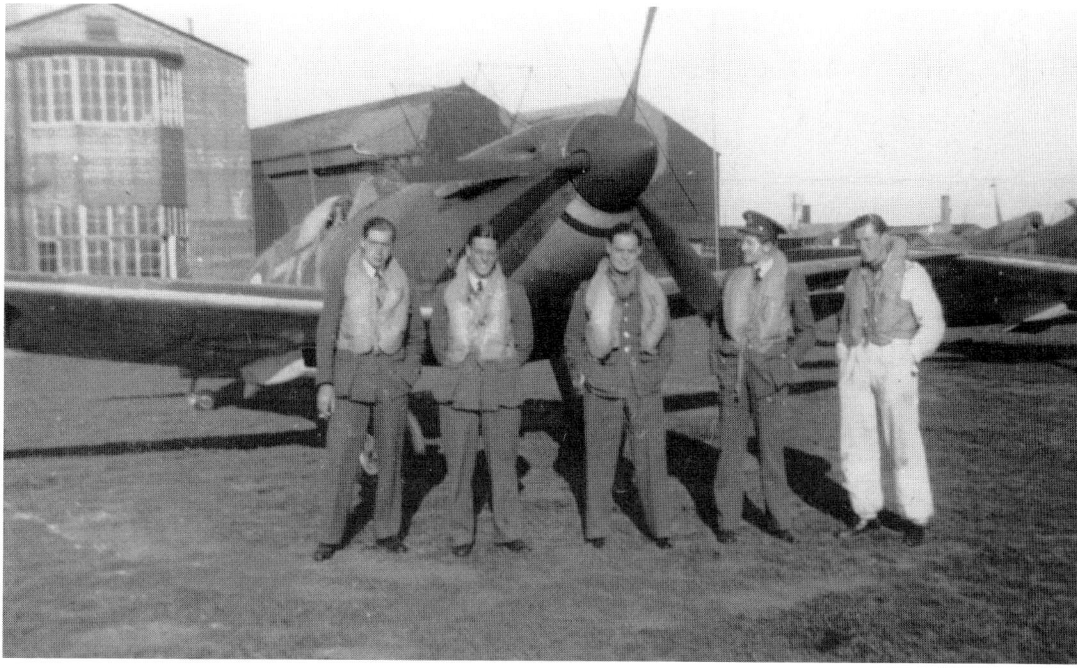

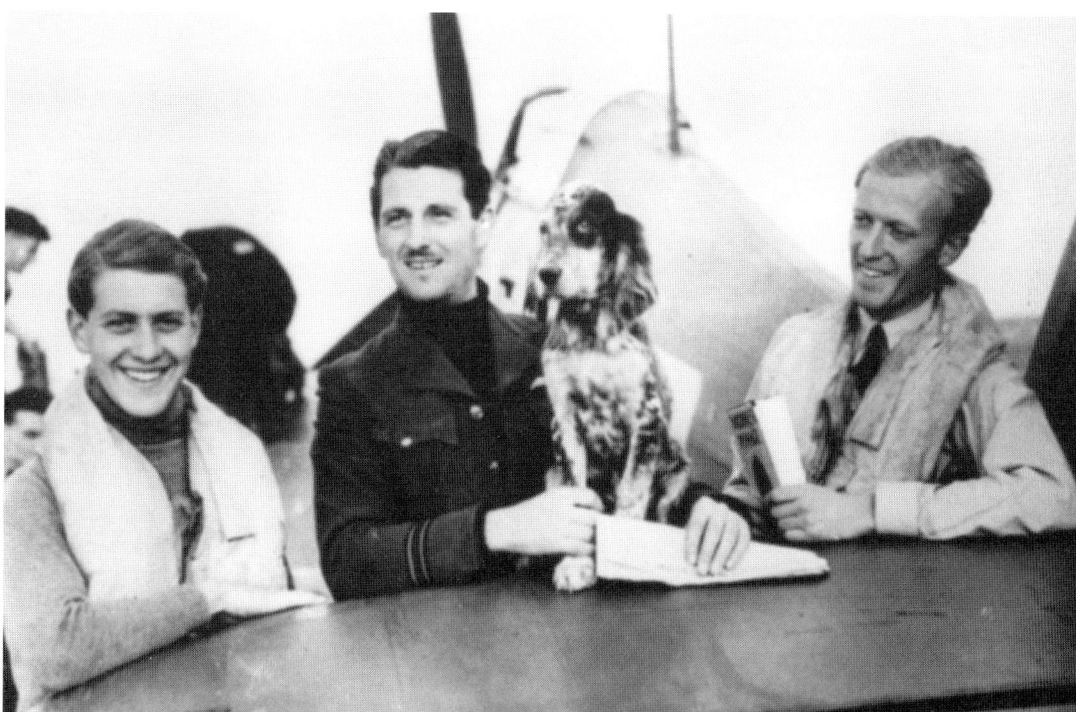

Above: In this posed photograph, the British commander of 310 Squadron, Squadron Leader Douglas Blackwood, confers over a map with Flight Lieutenant Sinclair DFC and Czech pilots, including, back row, from left, Sergeants Bohumir Furst, Rudolf Zima and Raimond Puda. To Blackwood's right is an unidentified sergeant; between Blackwood and Sinclair is Pilot Officer Vic Bergman, and finally another unidentified pilot. 310 Squadron flew in the controversial Duxford 'Big Wing'.

Opposite: Pilot Officer Arthur Vokes, an RAFVR pilot on 19 Squadron at Fowlmere, flying Spitfires, who had been a bank clerk before the war in Birmingham. A member of 'A' Flight, he flew throughout the Battle of Britain and eventually took over the Squadron after Squadron Leader Jack Lawson DFC was killed on 28 August 1941. The following day, Vokes led a flight of Spitfires to search for their missing CO over the North Sea running into a gaggle of Me 110s and, surprisingly, coming off second best: four Spitfires were lost. Flight Lieutenant Vokes survived that action but was killed a week later when he flew into the ground in bad visibility near Langham aerodrome.

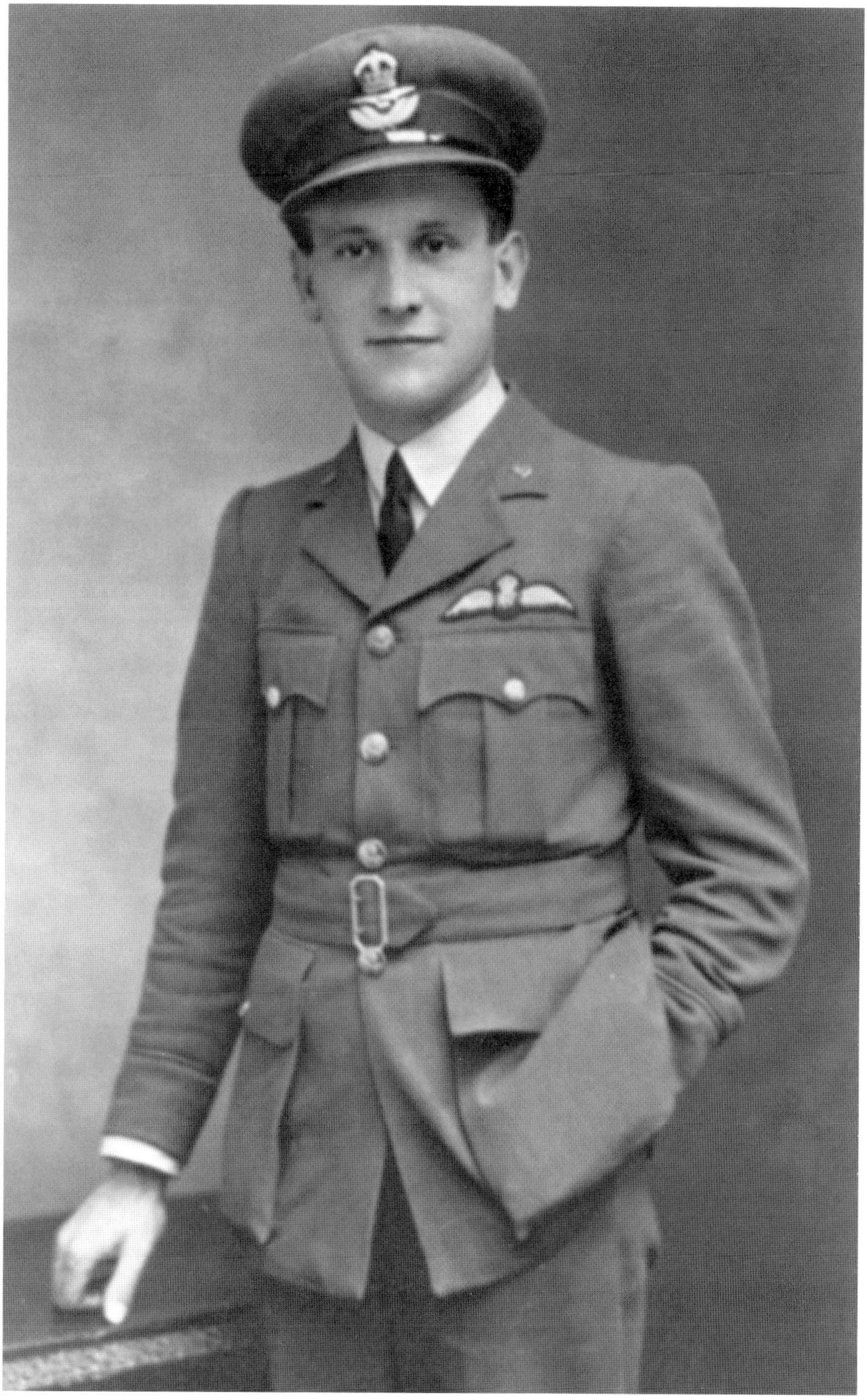

An Old Malvernian, Denis Crowley-Milling was a Rolls-Royce apprentice before the war who learned to fly with the RAFVR. During the Battle of Britain he flew Hurricanes with Squadron Leader Bader's 242 Squadron, often as his wingman. Having survived being shot-up on 7 September 1940, 'Crow' became a highly decorated ace and made a 'Home Run' across the Pyrenees, helped with the French Resistance, after being shot down flying Spitfires over the continent in 1941. He subsequently commanded one of the first Typhoon squadrons and, remaining in the post war service, rose to Air Marshal; he died on 1 December 1996. A great friend and supporter of the author, his story appears in *Letters From The Few* (2020).

Above: Gerald Edge (right) was a pre-war auxiliary who saw extensive action in both the Fall of France and Battle of Britain, becoming an ace, flying Hurricanes with 605 and 253 Squadrons, the latter which he commanded at Kenley. Awarded the DFC, he survived the war, leaving the service as a group captain in 1945. After farming in Kenya, Gerry settled in Astwood Bank, Worcestershire, and died in 2000.

Right: Peter Olver was also a pre-war volunteer reservist who converted to Spitfires whilst the Battle of Britain was at its height. Posted to 603 Squadron at Hornchurch as a replacement pilot on 19 October 1940, he was shot down six days later on his first and only operational sortie during the Battle of Britain and baled out, wounded. He returned to operational flying and later became an ace over the Western Desert and Mediterranean before being shot down and captured over Sicily. Peter survived the war and also farmed in Kenya afterwards, before returning to Devon; he died in February 2013.

Wing Commander Eric Thomas DSO DFC was a pre-war officer and amongst the very first Spitfire pilots when 19 Squadron received R.J. Mitchell's new fighter in 1938. For most of the Battle of Britain he was a flight commander on 222 Squadron, another rising ace awarded the DFC, and later a DSO for his leadership of the Biggin Hill Wing. His was an impressive operational career – but, somewhat surprisingly, his story is little-known and hence its inclusion, in detail, in the author's *Forgotten Heroes of the Battle of Britain* (2022). Having been invalided out of the service in 1944, suffering from TB, the disease ultimately claimed his life prematurely in 1972. Eric is pictured here with his personal Spitfire Mk IX whilst leading the Biggin Hill Wing.

Like the Poles, Czech pilots also flew in British squadrons: this is 19 Squadron's Pilot Officer Frantisek Hradil at Fowlmere in his Spitfire Mk IIA at Fowlmere in late 1940. He had previously served in the Czech Air Force before the war, and initially flew Hurricanes with 310 Squadron before converting to Spitfires and moving across to 19 Squadron in August 1940. He damaged an Me 109 on 27 September 1940 – but was killed in action over the Thames Estuary on 5 November 1940. He was 28 years old and was buried in Southend – a long way from home.

At the start of the Battle of Britain, 19 Squadron was commanded by Squadron Leader Phillip Pinkham AFC, a pre-war pilot who had previously instructed on Hurricanes. Pinkham was in a difficult position because his Squadron was operating the experimental cannon-armed Spitfire Mk IB, which was troublesome indeed owing to frequent stoppages, and so developing tactics around this type and resolving the issues arising took much of his time. Consequently he did not meet the enemy until 5 September 1940 – when he was shot down attacking a German bomber over Kent and killed.

Flight Sergeant Harry Steere was a pre-war Halton apprentice and NCO who was able to become a fighter pilot owing to the 1936 Expansion Plan. An ace awarded the DFM, along with his great friend Flight Sergeant George Unwin, at 26 years old, Steere was considered too old for single-seater fighter operations after the Battle of Britain and became an instructor. Eventually the pair managed to return to 'ops', flying night-intruder Mosquitos during the D-Day period – but Flight Lieutenant Steere, as he was by then, was shot down over Rennes and killed on 9 June 1944.

Flying Officer Leonard Haines was another ace on 19 Squadron during the Battle of Britain who was awarded the DFC. Shortly after getting married, however, whilst serving as a flying instructor at Heston, he and his passenger were killed as the result of unauthorised low-level aerobatics on 30 April 1941.

Pilot Officer Eric Burgoyne, also of 19 Squadron, was shot down and killed in combat with Me 109s on 27 September 1940. He is buried at St Mary's, Burghfield, Berkshire.

Flight Lieutenant Richard Hellyer was a pre-war auxiliary pilot and a founder member of 616 'South Yorkshire' Squadron in 1938. During Operation DYNAMO he was shot down and forced-landed on Dunkirk beach before returning to England. During the Squadron's disastrous Kenley deployment he shared a Ju 88, then became a flying instructor. Leaving the RAF in 1945, Hellyer lived in South Africa until his death on 28 October 1995 – he was then brought back to England and buried at St Andrew's, Tangmere.

Above: Wing Commander Francis Victor Beamish (left) was an RAF legend. A pre-war Cranwellian who commanded North Weald during the Battle of Britain, Beamish continued flying operationally with his station's fighter squadrons, becoming an ace and adding the DSO and DFC to his existing AFC. Further success followed in 1941 and 1942, until that fateful day, 29 March 1942, when he disappeared over the Channel whilst leading the Kenley Wing. Beamish is seen here with Flight Lieutenant Ian 'Widge' Gleed DFC, who later commanded 87 Squadron but was ultimately killed in action over Tunisia on 16 April 1943, by which time he was also a wing commander decorated with the DSO. The photograph was taken at Colerne on 7 February 1941, when Beamish flew a P-40 in a mock dogfight with Gleed's Hurricane.

Opposite above: Another of 'Rubber' Thorogood's snapshots, 'Widge' Gleed is seen here in his personal Hurricane at Bibury during the Battle of Britain.

Opposite below: Two auxiliary Spitfire pilots of 609 'West Riding' Squadron pictured at Warmwell during the Battle of Britain. At left is Pilot Officer David Crook DFC, an ace eventually reported missing off the Scottish coast in a photographic reconnaissance Spitfire on 18 December 1944. A married man with two children, Crook left behind his classic memoir, *Spitfire Pilot*, the original manuscript of which, with extra photographs and commentary by this author, was published by Pen & Sword in 2021. At right is Pilot Officer Geoffrey Gaunt, reputedly a cousin of Hollywood star James Mason, who was shot down over London in flames on 15 September 1940.

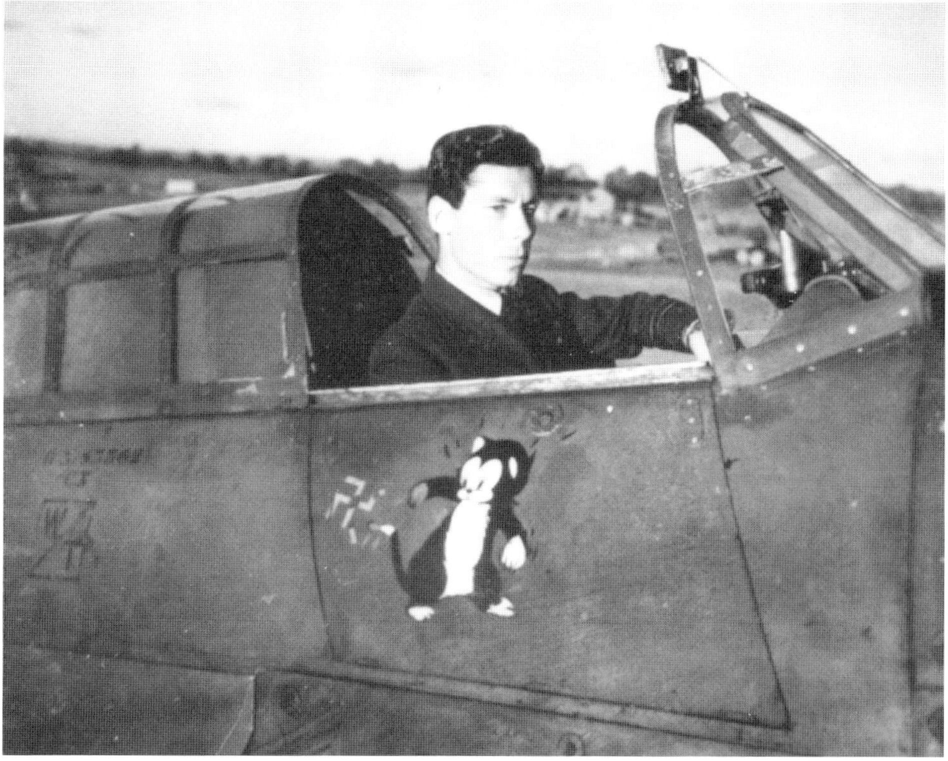

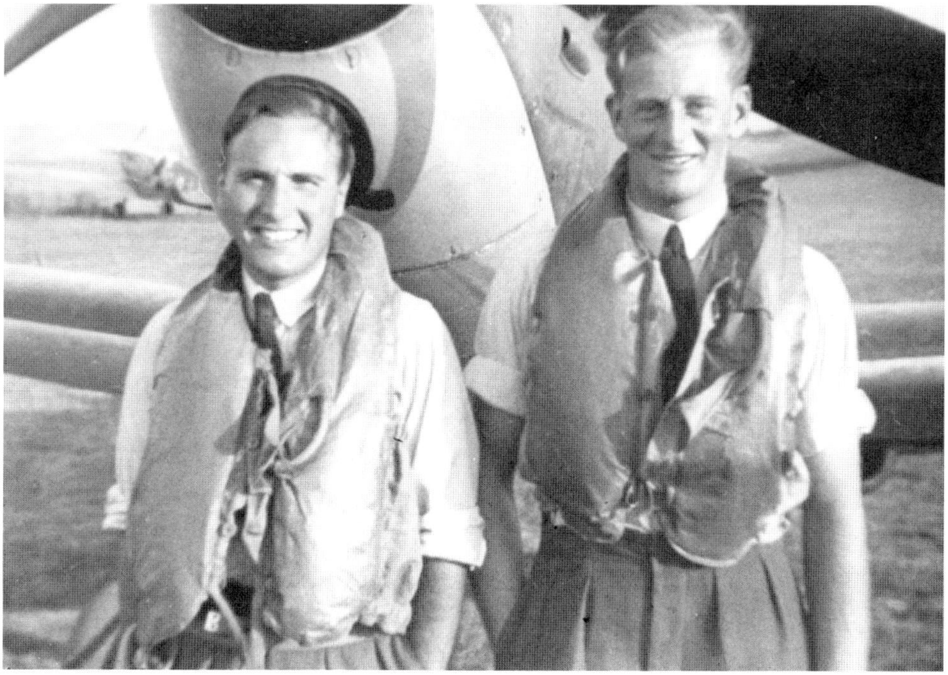

Another 609 Squadron pilot to lose his life in action during the Battle of Britain was Pilot Officer Rogers Miller, who collided head-on with an Me 110 over Dorchester on 27 September 1940. The previous month, his brother, Pilot Officer John Miller, a Wellington pilot, was killed in a landing mishap at Stradishall. The Millers' full story is told in the author's *Battle of Britain 1940: The Finest Hour's Human Cost* (2020).

The Polish commander of 303 Squadron, shadowing his British counterpart Ronald Kellett, was Squadron Leader Zdiszlaw Krasnodebski, pictured here at Northolt after the Battle of Britain. On 6 September 1940, he was shot down and badly burned, requiring treatment by Sir Archibald McIndoe at the famed Burns Unit of the Royal Victoria Hospital, East Grinstead. A 'Guinea Pig', he is the 'Poley Boy' referred to by Tom Gleave in *I Had A Row With A German*, published in 1941. Krasnodebski survived the war and died in Canada in 1980.

Flying Officer C.O.J. 'Joe' Pegge flew Spitfires with 610 Squadron and became an ace during the Battle of Britain, decorated with the DFC. Awarded a Bar to his DFC whilst commanding 607 Squadron in Burma during 1944, Squadron Leader Pegge survived the war but was killed on 9 May 1950 when his Meteor jet crashed into the Wash in bad weather.

Squadron Leader Herbert 'Pinners' Pinfold was a pre-war officer and experienced pilot who was given command of 56 Squadron, flying Hurricanes, on 31 August 1940. Permanently commissioned the following month, he subsequently served as an instructor and staff officer, retiring as a group captain in 1958. The story of his escapade on 30 September 1940, when he was shot-up by a German bomber and narrowly survived a hasty forced-landing, is told in the author's *Letters From The Few* (2020); he died on 19 October 2009.

Flight Sergeant Peter Morfill was another pre-war Halton apprentice, otherwise known in the service as a 'Trenchard Brat', who qualified as a flight rigger and made the quantum leap to fighter pilot. After training, he joined 65 Squadron at Hornchurch in 1937, first flying Hawker Fury biplanes before converting to Spitfires, and is pictured there at that time. Peter saw action flying Hurricanes with 501 Squadron during the Fall of France and Battle of Britain, receiving the DFM. Afterwards he served overseas as a flying instructor, remaining in the post-war service until retiring as a squadron leader in 1958. He died on 3 April 2004.

A pre-war volunteer reservist and lawyer, Pilot Officer Harold Goodall was posted to fly the ill-fated Boulton-Paul Defiant turret-fighter with 264 Squadron at Duxford on 22 May 1940. There he teamed up with an air-gunner from New Zealand, Sergeant-Observer Robert Bett Mirk Young. Sadly, the Defiant squadrons would suffer such grievous losses during the Battle of Britain that the type was withdrawn from the daylight fighting. Goodall and Young survived these battles, however, claiming German bombers destroyed on 24 and 26 August 1940. Ironically, they were shot down by a German bomber at night, on 8 October 1940, and were killed. Pilot Officer Goodall was buried at Parkstone Cemetery, Poole.

Sergeant-Observer Robert Bett Mirk Young of Palmerston North, New Zealand, Pilot Officer Goodall's air-gunner, who was buried at Northwood – a long way from home. The story of this unfortunate Defiant crew is told in the author's *Battle of Britain 1940: The Finest Hour's Human Cost* (2020).

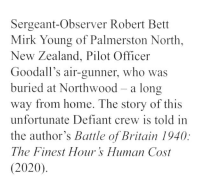

Sergeant George Richard 'Dick' Collett was an Etonian who became a volunteer reservist in March 1939. After training and conversion to Spitfires, Dick was posted to 54 Squadron at Rochford on 15 July 1940. Having destroyed an Me 109 on 24 July, he ran out of petrol and forced-landed on the beach at Dunwich, writing-off his Spitfire. On 22 August 1940, he was shot down into the Channel and killed whilst defending Convoy TOTEM. Buried at Bergen-Op-Zoom, Netherlands, the full story is included in *Battle of Britain 1940: The Finest Hour's Human Cost* (2020).

Hugh Reilley was one of over 100 Canadians amongst The Few, who saw action flying Spitfires with 66 Squadron from Gravesend. After several aerial victories, Reilley was shot down and killed on 17 October 1940 in combat with Me 109s over Kent, most likely by Major Werner Mölders, Kommodore of JG 51. Again, his full story is told in the author's *Battle of Britain 1940: The Finest Hour's Human Cost* (2020).

Pilot Officer Martyn Aurel King has the distinction of being both the youngest of the Few, born on 15 October 1921, and youngest to be killed in action during the Battle of Britain. Brought up by missionary parents in China, on 16 August 1940 he was flying in the section of three 249 Squadron Hurricanes led by Flight Lieutenant James Nicolson and patrolling over Southampton. The British fighters were bounced by Me 109s, Nicolson being shot down in flames but refusing to bale out until he had attacked his assailant. King's aircraft was hit, forcing him to bale out, but unfortunately shrapnel had badly damaged his parachute, as a result of which the canopy collapsed; the teenage pilot died in the arms of a passing Sotonian in a Southampton garden. It was originally believed that Nicolson's section had been attacked by Me 110s, and eyewitnesses claimed that King had been machine-gunned on his parachute. More recent information, from his newly released casualty file, however, confirmed that Me 109s were responsible and that King's parachute had been damaged in the initial attack. Nicolson, of course, was awarded the VC for his 'signal act of valour' that day, the only RAF fighter pilot so recognised during the Second World War.

Above left: Sergeant Peter McIntosh grew up close to Croydon airport and was fascinated by aviation from an early age. In February 1939 he joined the RAFVR, and saw action during the Battle of Britain with 151 and 605 Squadrons. On 12 October 1940, Peter was with the latter and based at Croydon, close to home. That day, however, he was reported missing following a skirmish with Me 109s over Kent, another victim of Major Mölders. The crash-site of his Hurricane was only found and identified by the efforts of Peter's father and brother, who travelled to and made their own enquiries in the area where the combat took place. Consequently, Peter's body was recovered from the crash-site on Littlestone Golf Course and brought home for burial at Shirley Cemetery, Croydon. Again, the full story appears in the author's *Battle of Britain 1940: The Finest Hour's Human Cost* (2020).

Above right: The South African Adolph Gysbert Malan emerged as the greatest RAF fighter leader during the early war period, whose score of thirty-two enemy aircraft destroyed was only exceeded in 1944 by Wing Commander Johnnie Johnson. Universally known as 'Sailor', having originally served as a mercantile naval officer, Malan, who made the Spitfire's first nocturnal kill on 19 June 1940, commanded 74 'Tiger' Squadron in the Battle of Britain, and went on to lead the Biggin Hill Wing until going into training in August 1941. After the war, by which time he was a highly decorated group captain, 'Sailor' returned to South Africa, with his wife and two children, to farm at Slent. Opposed to any kind of injustice, he became an anti-apartheid activist and president of the 'Torch Commando', comprising ex-servicemen opposed to this deplorable racism, but tragically died prematurely, aged 52, of Parkinson's. The author is his most recent biographer, *Sailor Malan: Freedom Fighter* having been produced with the pilot's close family's full support.

114

Two of Sailor Malan's most successful fighter pilots on 74 Squadron were Pilot Officer Harbourne Mackay Stephen (left), yet another pre-war volunteer reservist, and Flying Officer John Colin Mingo-Park (right). The pair are pictured here on 30 November 1940, having minutes previously shared in the destruction of a Me 109 – Biggin Hill's 600th victory. Mungo-Park was subsequently awarded the DFC and Bar, succeeding Malan in command of the 'Tigers' before being killed in action over France on 27 June 1941; his final score was eleven and two shared destroyed, five probables and four damaged. Stephen received the first immediate award of the DSO to an airman, in addition to the DFC and Bar, surviving the war accredited with nine destroyed and four shared, three probables and another shared, and seven damaged. After the war he held senior positions on Fleet Street, being made a CBE in 1985; he died on 22 August 2001.

Sergeant Tony Mould was also a reservist serving with 74 Squadron. His first victory was recorded over Dunkirk on 22 May 1940, and two days later he survived being shot down over France, coming home by boat. He is best remembered for shooting down the first German fighter to crash in England during the war, on 8 July 1940, an Me 109 of JG 51. After several other successes he was again shot down, baling out wounded. Later commissioned, he also fought with the 'Tigers' in 1941, but was killed whilst serving with 85 Squadron on 20 January 1943, when his Mosquito crashed into Bradwell Bay.

The shortage of trained pilots to replace casualties after the Fall of France, in anticipation of the defence of Britain ahead, led to Fighter Command's ranks being swelled by pilots who volunteered from other commands and services. These are two of the fifty-seven Fleet Air Arm pilots amongst The Few, namely Sub-Lieutenants Richard 'Dickie' Cork (left) and Richard Gardner, both of whom flew Hurricanes in Squadron Leader Douglas Bader's famous 242 Squadron. Cork was a professional, indicated by his sleeve rank ring being a straight line, whereas Gardner was a reservist of the so-called 'Wavy Navy', owing to the zig-zag sleeve ring of the RNVR. Both became successful fighter pilots, but only Gardner survived the war: Cork was killed on 14 April 1944 in a flying accident whilst serving in the Far East on HMS *Illustrious*.

Above: Another regular FAA officer amongst The Few is 19 Squadron's Sub-Lieutenant Arthur 'Admiral' Blake, a popular member of the Squadron killed in action over Chelmsford on 29 October 1940 – six other naval pilots lost their lives in the Battle of Britain.

Opposite: Flight Lieutenant Percy 'Squeak' Weaver was initially commissioned into the reserve of RAF Officers in early 1937, joining 56 Squadron at North Weald; he then took a Short Service Commission and by February 1940 was serving as an Operations Room Controller, also at North Weald. In June 1940, by now a most experienced officer and pilot, he re-joined 56 Squadron, becoming an ace in the first half of the Battle of Britain. A great support to the Squadron's new commander, Squadron Leader G.A.L. 'Minnie' Manton, 'Squeak' was a highly popular and able flight commander – but was shot down over the Essex coast and reported missing on 31 August 1940. As his body was never recovered, Flight Lieutenant Weaver is commemorated on the Runnymede Memorial. His DFC was gazetted on 1 October 1940, and, again, the full story is told in *Battle of Britain 1940: The Final Hour's Human Cost* (2020).

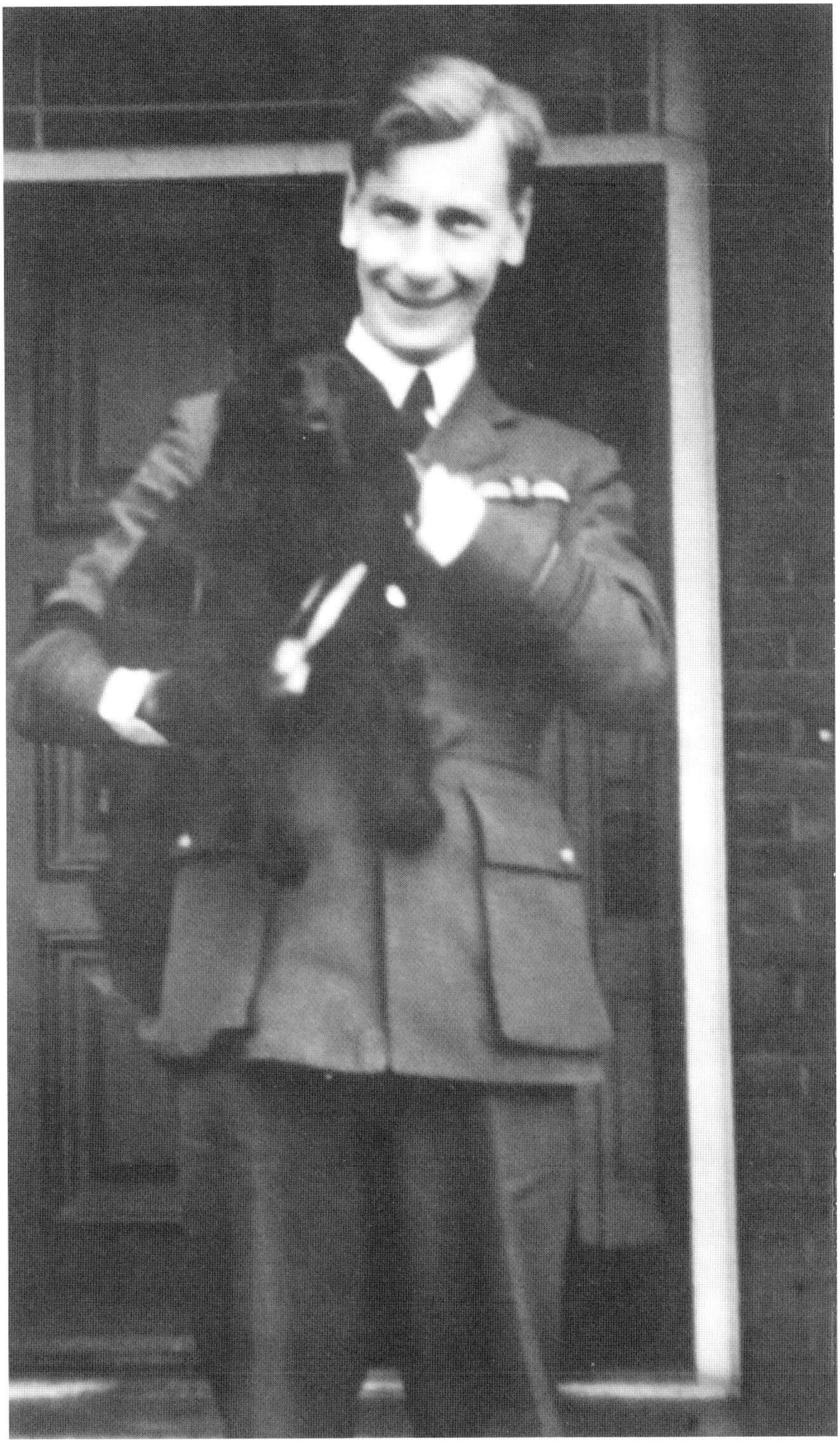

Above: Another 56 Squadron stalwart was Flight Sergeant Frederick 'Taffy' Higginson, a professional airman later commissioned and seen here at 'readiness' during the Battle of Britain at North Weald. 'Taffy' became an early ace, was awarded the DFM and, after being shot down over France, made a 'Home Run' in 1941. Decorated with the DFC, he enjoyed a long and varied career, remaining in the service until 1956. Afterwards he worked for Bristol Aircraft and retired to St Clears, near Tenby in South Wales. Wing Commander F.W. Higginson OBE DFC DFM died on 12 February 2003. His story is also included in *Letters From The Few* (2020).

Opposite above: From left: Flying Officer Barry Sutton, Flight Lieutenant Eustace 'Gus' Holden, and Pilot Officer Peter Down, all of 56 Squadron, pictured at North Weald. All three survived the war, although Sutton was shot down, possibly accidentally by a Spitfire, on 28 August 1940 and badly burned. He was another pilot featured in the excellent John Willis documentary *Churchill's Few*.

Right: The south-west, defended by Air Vice-Marshal Sir Quentin Brand's 10 Group, also saw heavy fighting, especially over the Portland and Weymouth areas. Based just inland, at Warmwell, was 152 Squadron, one of the unit's foremost pilots being Pilot Officer Eric 'Boy' Marrs. A Cranwellian, Marrs became an ace, receiving the DFC in January 1941, but was shot down by flak and killed during a low-level attack on Brest, 24 July 1941.

Flight Sergeant Eric Williams was a professional pre-war airman and another Halton apprentice who became a fighter pilot. During the Battle of Britain he flew Hurricanes with 46 Squadron, damaging a Do 17 on 2 September 1940 but shot-up himself the following day and slightly wounded. On 15 October 1940, Williams was shot down over the Thames Estuary. Although reported missing and his body never recovered, it is known that his aircraft crashed in Gravesend, burying it deep into the water table in a warehouse adjacent to the Thames. The nature of the site defied recovery at the time, and since, so the pilot is commemorated on the Runnymede Memorial.

Pilot Officer Byron 'Ron' Duckenfield was a pre-war regular airman who passed aptitude tests and successfully trained to be a fighter pilot. Commissioned, he was injured during the Fall of France when the Bombay aircraft transporting him and other passengers to the continent crashed on landing. Consequently, he did not join 501 until 23 July 1940, but was soon in action, destroying several enemy aircraft. By February 1942 he was commanding 615 Squadron, with which he served in the Far East before suffering engine-failure attacking a Japanese-held airfield, and captured. Surviving the experience, Group Captain Duckenfield eventually retired from the service in 1969; he died on 19 November 2010.

Above: Hurricane pilot Flight Lieutenant Peter Gardner DFC snapped by Flight Lieutenant Peter Brothers DFC outside the 32 Squadron pilots' hut at Acklington, sometime after the Squadron had been withdrawn there on 27 August 1940. Another successful fighter pilot of the Battle of Britain period, Gardner was shot down flying Spitfires with 54 Squadron the following year and captured; he died in 1984.

Opposite: Squadron Leader Mike Crossley, who commanded 32 Squadron during the Battle of Britain, was an exceptional fighter pilot and leader, his efforts during the Fall of France recognised with a DFC in June 1940, followed by appointment to the DSO in August for his inspirational leadership of 32 Squadron during the first half of the Battle of Britain. He survived the war but died suddenly in South Africa during 1987.

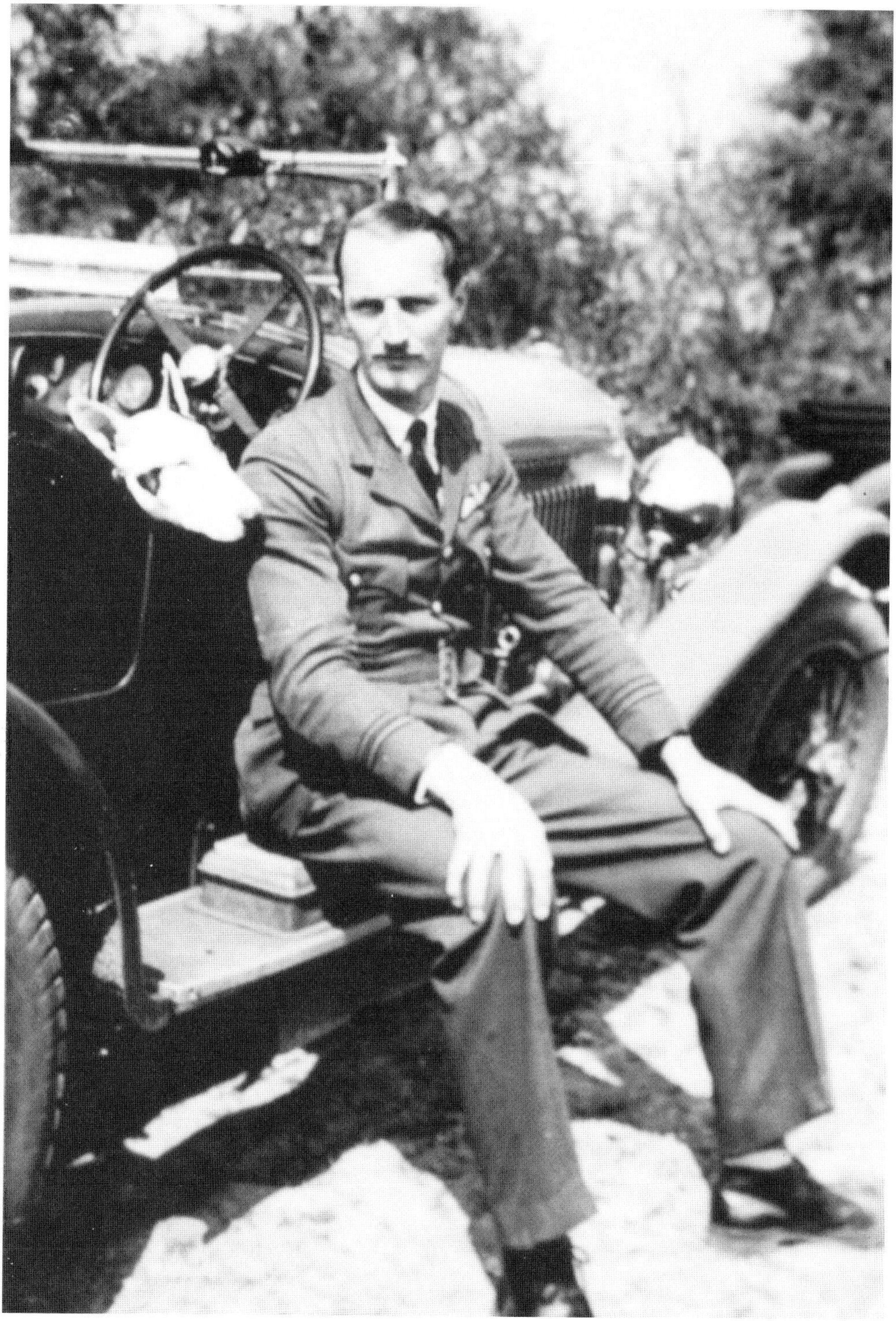

Pilot Officer Karol Pniak was also amongst the first free Poles to reach England, a 30-year-old career officer posted initially to 32 Squadron, who had seen action during the all too brief battle for his homeland. He destroyed a number of enemy aircraft in the Battle of Britain, and later over the Western Desert. After the war he returned to Poland and died there in 1980.

Pilot Officer George Drake was a South African who answered the call and travelled to England to take a Short Service Commission in 1939. After training he joined 607 Squadron at Usworth, going south with the Squadron, to Tangmere, on 1 September 1940. Reported missing after a combat eight days later, his remains were not recovered until his Hurricane's crash-site was excavated at Goudhurst, Kent, in 1972. In fact, Drake was the first of the 'Missing Few' to be discovered by amateur aviation archaeology enthusiasts post-war. He was given a full military funeral at Brookwood Cemetery on 22 November 1972.

Above: Sergeant Denis Helcke was an aeronautical engineering graduate who gained his civilian pilot's licence before joining the RAFVR in March 1939. On 7 September 1940, he was flying Hurricanes with 504 Squadron, based at Hendon, and destroyed a He 111. Ten days later, however, he lost control of his aircraft during a practice flight and was killed; although Helcke baled out, he fell dead at Selling, having possibly struck the doomed Hurricane.

Opposite: Aleksander Gabszewicz was a legendary Polish fighter leader who had shared a He 111 destroyed over Poland on the first day of the Second World War. He scored again whilst flying with the French Air Force, but did not add to his score during the Battle of Britain, during which he flew in the latter days with 607 Squadron. In November 1940, Flying Officer Gabszewicz joined 303 (Polish) Squadron and ultimately became a highly respected wing leader, decorated with the DSO, DFC, and various Polish gallantry awards. After the war, he settled in England, and died in Malvern, Worcestershire, on 10 October 1983.

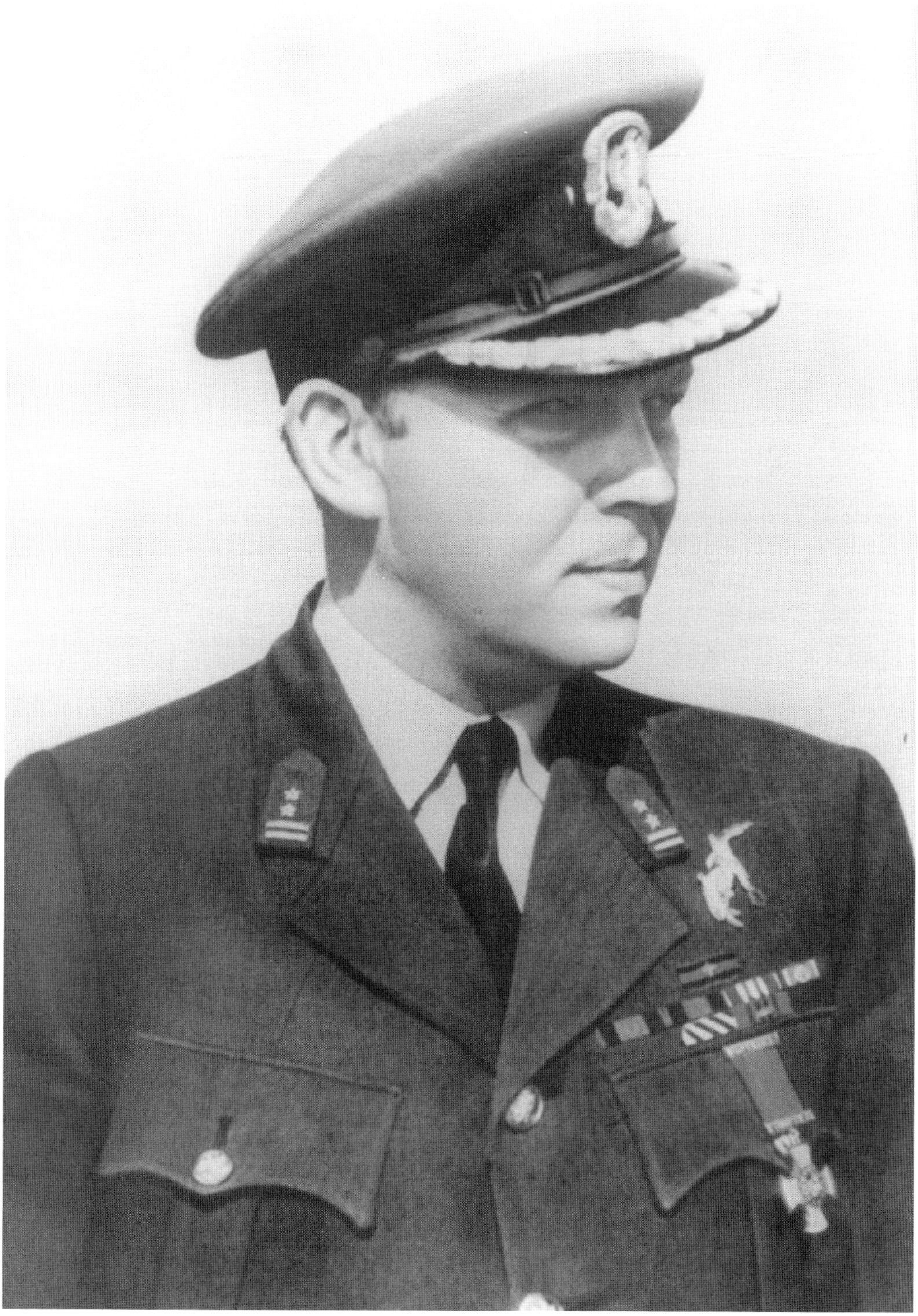

Eddie Egan learned to fly before the war, soloing aged 17. Another reservist, on 15 September 1940 he destroyed a Me 109 whilst flying Hurricanes from Kenley with 501 Squadron. Two days later he was patrolling over Ashford with Sergeant Tony Pickering when the pair were bounced by high-flying Me 109s, and Sergeant Egan was shot down. Although Pickering reported the crash-site location, Sergeant Egan's remains were not recovered until 1976, by aviation archaeology enthusiasts. The pilot was not identified, however, until after the site was investigated again in 1976. Sergeant Eddie Egan is buried at Brookwood.

RAF Northolt accommodated both 1 Squadron RAF and, confusingly, 1 Squadron RCAF, during the Battle of Britain, both of which flew Hurricanes. This is the Canadian Pilot Officer Peter de Peyster Brown of the latter unit, at Northolt during the summer of 1940. He made several combat claims during the summer of 1940, transferring to the American Air Force in 1942.

Another 1 RCAF Squadron snapshot from Northolt days: Flying Officers Arthur 'Art' Yuile and Blair Dalzel 'Dal' Russell. Both became successful fighter pilots, especially Russell, who became a highly decorated and distinguished fighter leader.

Above: Flying Officer Arthur Deane Nesbitt of 1 RCAF Squadron, also at Northolt – note the 'Canada' shoulder flash. Another successful and decorated Canadian pilot who survived the war, Nesbitt died on 22 February 1978 from injuries sustained in a skiing accident.

Opposite above: Flying Officer Nesbitt pictured at Prestwick, Scotland, before the Battle of Britain.

Opposite below: Flying Officer 'Art' Yuile, also at Prestwick.

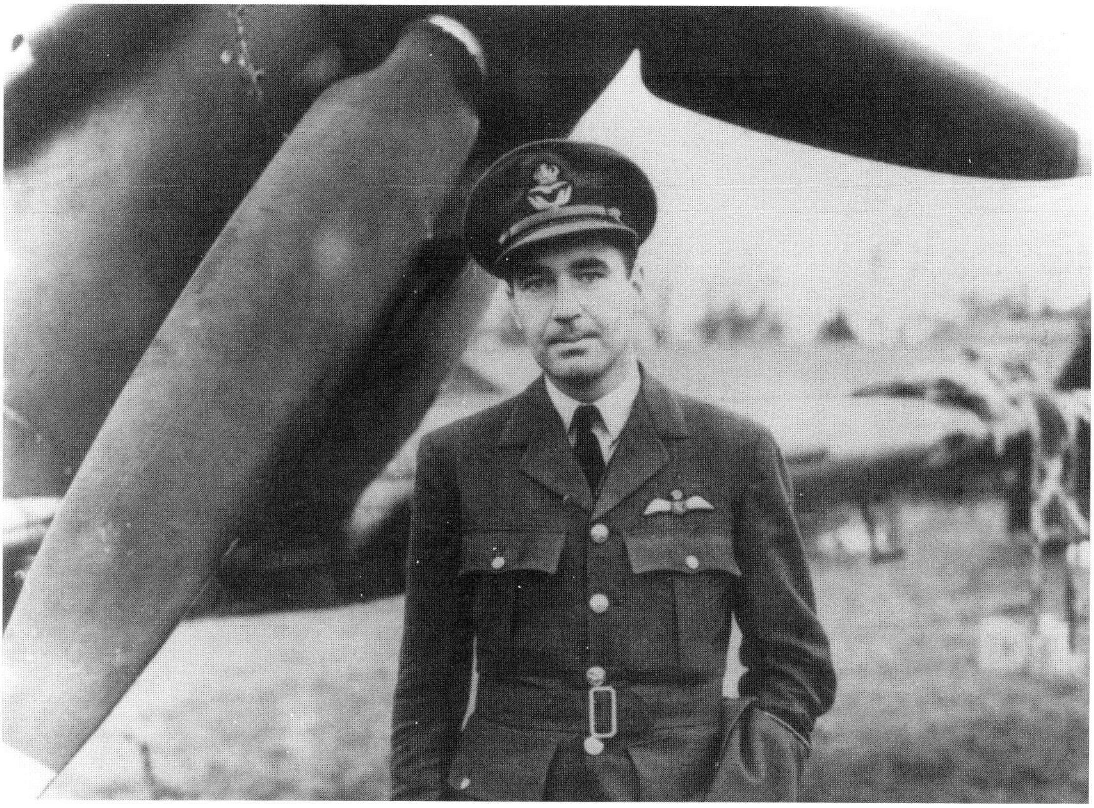

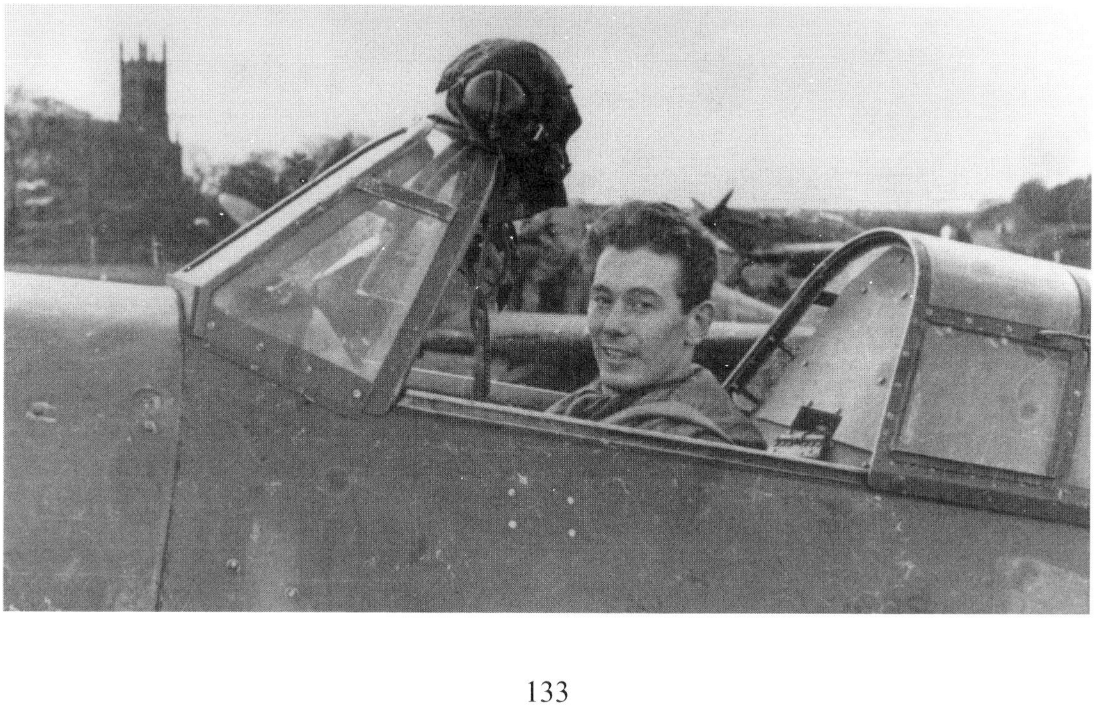

Denys Gillam was a pre-war officer and pilot who commanded 'B' Flight of 616 Squadron during the Battle of Britain. During the unit's disastrous deployment to Kenley, it was Gillam who held the Squadron together and recorded most of its victories during that period. Later, he became a low-level fighter-bombing specialist and survived the war a highly decorated group captain; he died in 1991.

Two more reservists mobilised upon outbreak of war, namely Pilot Officers Peter Hairs (left) and Gordon Parkin of 501 Squadron, pictured at Le Mans, France, during June 1940. Hairs saw action over France, but Parkin arrived shortly before the Squadron was brought home and badly injured at Gravesend in a take-off accident on 30 July 1940. He never flew operationally again, serving as an instructor throughout the rest of the war, which both men survived. Gordon Parkin died on 23 July 1998, Peter Hairs on 24 August 2014.

Flight Lieutenant Richard Carew Reynell, known to all as 'Dick', was an Australian scholar at Oxford and member of the University Air Squadron, who took a Short Service Commission in 1931. During the Battle of Britain, he was a Hawker test pilot seconded to fly Hurricanes with 43 Squadron, based at Tangmere, on 26 August 1940. Over the next few days he scored a number of combat successes before being shot down and killed over South London on 7 September 1940. He is buried at Brookwood.

Squadron Leader Caesar Hull DFC, a South African, was posted to command 43 Squadron on 31 August 1940. A highly experienced and already successful fighter pilot, it is understood that although his ammunition was spent, he went to Flight Lieutenant Reynell's assistance, but was also shot down and killed in the process. The gallant Caesar was buried at St Andrew's, Tangmere.

Above: Another Australian to lose his life in the Battle of Britain was Flight Lieutenant Paterson Hughes DFC of 234 Squadron. An ace, he, like Dick Reynell, was killed on 7 September 1940, when his Spitfire either collided with or rammed the Do 17 he was attacking over Sundridge.

Left: John Hill took a Short Service Commission in 1932, so was an experienced pilot when he took over 504 Squadron in France, six days after the German invasion. Three days later his Hurricane was shot down; John baled out but was fired upon by French peasants armed with shotguns before being arrested and beaten up as a suspected German spy! Rescued by a French airman he made it home via Dunkirk, after more adventures. On 31 July 1940 he took command of 222 Squadron and destroyed several enemy aircraft during the unit's Hornchurch deployment in the Battle of Britain. He later served as a staff officer and eventually retired as a group captain in 1960 and died in 1998. This photograph was taken at Hornchurch during the summer of 1940.

More volunteer reservist, this time during training: Sergeants Denis 'Red' Parker (left), an unknown pilot, and Bob Poulton (right). All RAFVR pilots were automatically given the rank of sergeant, much to the displeasure of regular airmen who took years to reach that rank. Denis flew Spitfires towards the end of the Battle of Britain with 616 and 66 Squadron, and later saw action over Malta in 1942. Having instructed, he left the service in 1945, and died in 1998. See photographs 35/36 regarding Bob Poulton.

Above: 611 'West Lancashire' was an auxiliary fighter squadron, which saw action during the Battle of Britain when based in both 11 and 12 Groups. Certain pilots are snapped here at their Digby dispersal in August or September 1940; from left: Sergeant Levenson, Pilot Officer Jones, unknown, Pilot Officer MacFie, Pilot Officer Pollard, Flying Officer Watkins, Pilot Officer Scott-Malden, unknown, Pilot Officer Adams, Flying Officer Heath and Flight Lieutenant Stoddar; seated, smoking, is Flight Lieutenant Leather, and on the ground is Pilot Officer Brown.

Opposite above: In July 1940, one flight of 611 Squadron was detached to Ternhill, in Shropshire, where this snapshot was taken outside the squadron office, a bell tent formerly the property of 43 Squadron. The pilots, according to Pilot Officer Peter Brown (extreme left), were all badly hungover! Centre is Flight Lieutenant Leather, whilst on the grass, looking particular worse for wear, are Pilot Officers Sutton and Pollard.

Opposite below: Sergeant Robert Angus, a Scott, was yet another volunteer reservist who first served with 611 Squadron, then 41 Squadron at Hornchurch, where this snapshot was taken. On 20 February 1941, Angus became another victim of Major Werner Mölders when shot down over Dover; he baled out over the Channel but disappeared without a trace.

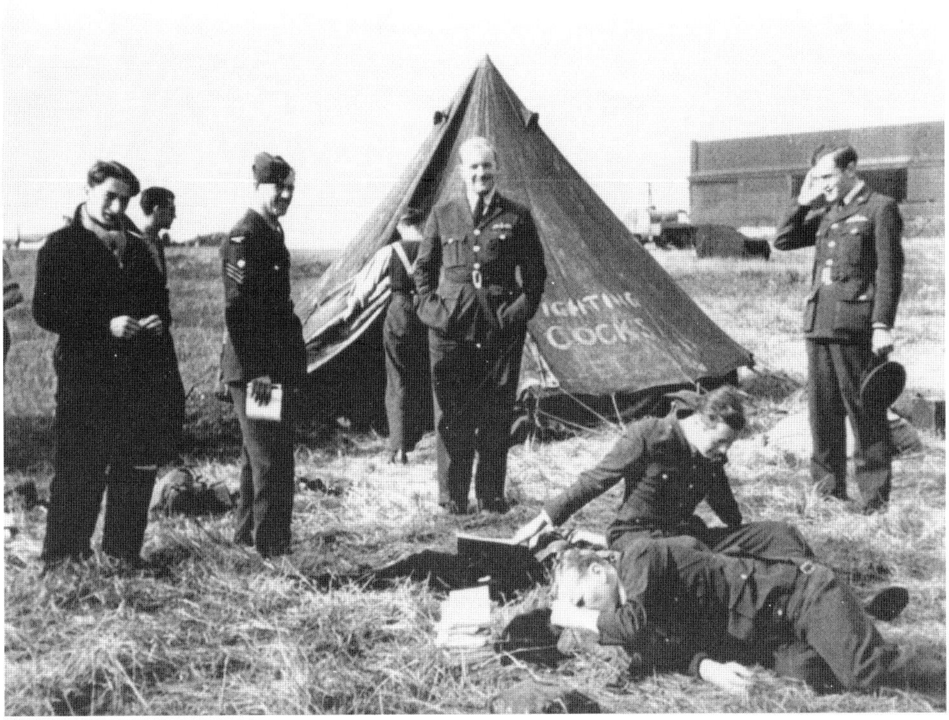
IGHTING
COCK

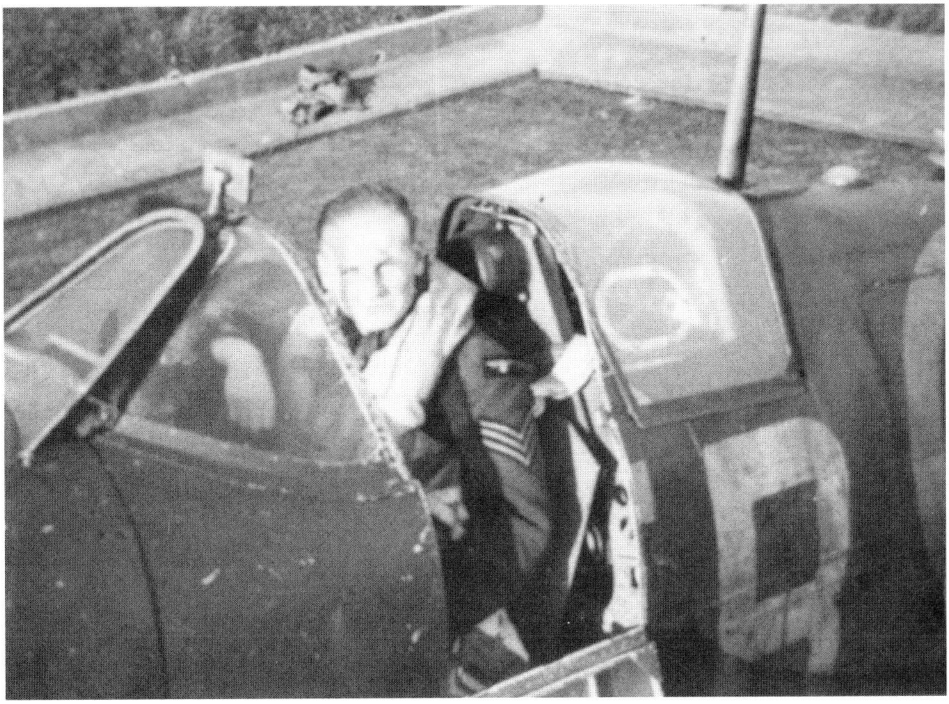

Archie 'Winkie' Winskill was also a reservist, commissioned in August 1940, who flew Spitfires during the Battle of Britain with 54, 72 and 603 Squadrons, becoming a flight commander on 41 Squadron at Hornchurch, where this snapshot was taken, in January 1941. On 14 August 1941 he was shot down over Calais, baled out and, with assistance from the French Resistance, made a home run. He subsequently became a squadron commander and increased his personal score fighting over North Africa. Remaining in the post-war service, he retired as an air commodore in 1968, after which he ran the Queen's Flight for several years. Awarded the DFC and Bar, Archie was knighted in 1980; he died in 2005.

Sergeant Edmund Shepperd was a pre-war airman and wireless mechanic selected for pilot training, joining 152 'Hyderabad' Squadron at Acklington in October 1939. He tasted combat early, damaging a He 111 reconnaissance bomber of 29 January 1940, and destroyed another on 3 February. After the Squadron went south, to Warmwell in Dorset, he destroyed several more enemy aircraft before crashing near Dorchester in bad visibility on 8 October 1940. The 23-year old pilot, pictured here at Warmwell with the Squadron mascot, 'Honorary Pilot Officer Pooch', was killed.

Above: Yet another volunteer reservist, Sergeant Kenneth Pattison, pictured with his wife, Joan, on honeymoon in Skegness. Pattison was posted to 611 Squadron on 27 September 1940, but whilst flying from Ternhill on 11 October 1940 became disorientated in a combat with Do 17s over Liverpool. Lost and in fading light, he made a wheels-up forced-landing at Cooksey Green in Worcestershire, but was fatally injured when the Spitfire hit a tree stump and cartwheeled. He died in Barnsley Hall Military Hospital, on 13 October 1940. Joan took him home to Nottingham, where Ken was buried at Nottingham Southern Cemetery.

Opposite above: Flying Officer Blair 'Crasher' White of 504 Squadron prepares for a sortie from Filton during the Battle of Britain – a successful fighter pilot ultimately reported missing over Sicily in 1943.

Opposite below: Flight Lieutenant Thomas Pugh DFC (left), Squadron Leader John Munro, and Flight Lieutenant D.A.C. Crooks DFC (right), three Westland Whirlwind pilots of 263 Squadron in early 1941. Pugh had previously flown Fairey Battle bombers during the Fall of France, and later commanded 263, which saw no action flying the so-called 'Crikey' during the Battle of Britain. He then formed 182 Squadron on the new Typhoon, which was initially problematic, but lost when the bomb beneath his aircraft prematurely exploded during a dive-bombing attack on Dieppe Harbour in 1943. Crooks, a Canadian, earned his DFC for daring low-level reconnaissance and bombing attacks during the Fall of France, but was not one of The Few; he failed to return from an operational flight, still with 263 Squadron, on 1 April 1941. No record exists of Munro having made an operational flight to qualify for the Battle of Britain Clasp, but following representation to the MOD by his son, the Clasp was awarded in 1981; Munro, however, died in 1951.

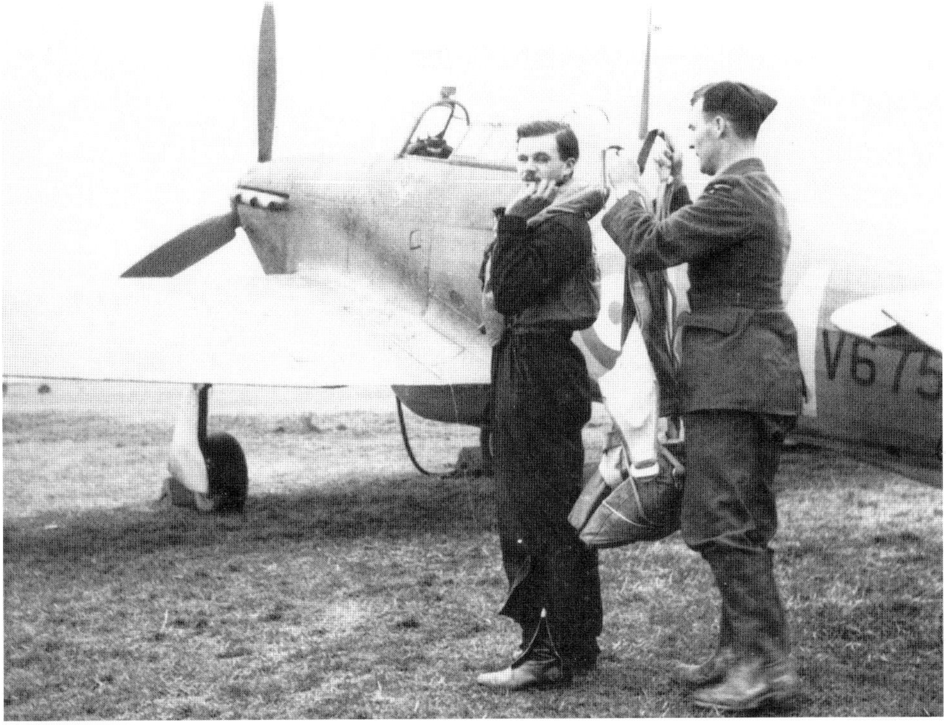
V675

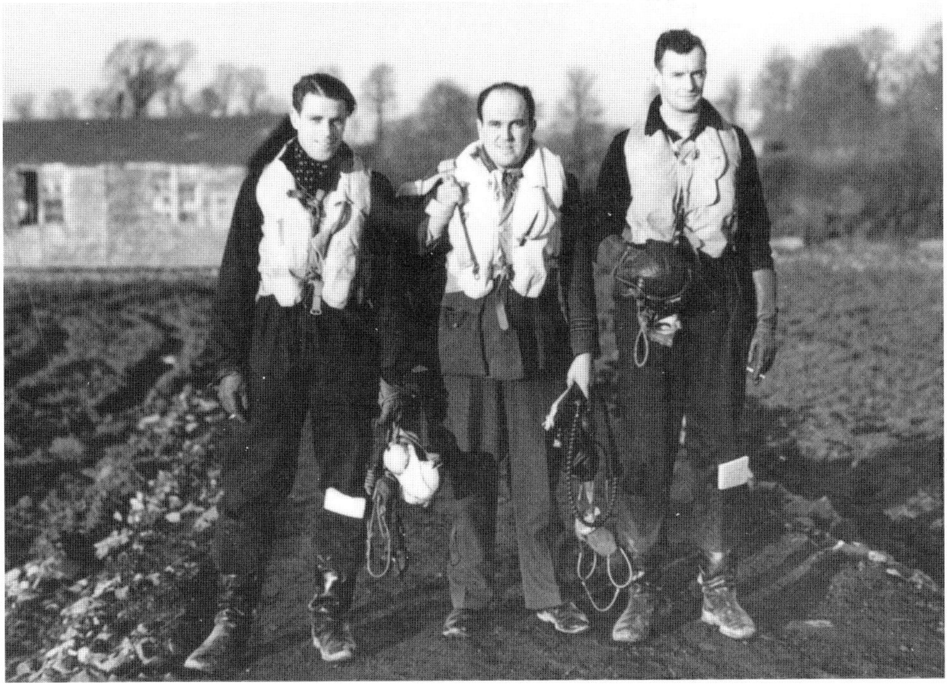

Above: Three pilots of 501 Squadron after the Battle of Britain (from left): Sergeant Tony Whitehouse, Pilot Officer Bob Dafforn and Sergeant Vic Ekins. The black flying suits were a pre-war affectation.

Opposite above: Flying Officer Dennis Williams (right), a Defiant pilot on 141 Squadron, with his air-gunner, Pilot Officer Geoffrey Pledger. The pair survived the Battle of Britain, during which their Squadron suffered ten fatal casualties. On 4 April 1941, the pair were recalled to Gravesend from a nocturnal patrol, due to deteriorating weather, but were killed when their Defiant flew into the ground in bad visibility.

Opposite below: Group Captain G.A.L. 'Minnie' Manton took a Short Service Commission in 1931, and was Permanently Commissioned in 1936. He converted to single-engine fighters in June 1940, but had only a few hours on Spitfires and Hurricanes, and no combat experience, when he was posted to command 56 Squadron at North Weald on 1 July 1940 – a not untypical scenario at the time. Over the next few weeks he claimed several German aircraft destroyed or as 'probables', and survived being shot-up and wounded. On 5 September 1940, promoted to wing commander, he took over RAF Manston, and later became Wing Leader at Northolt before, after non-operational postings, he commanded 907 fighter-bomber Wing in Burma, where this photograph was taken in 1944; he left the service in 1960, emigrated to Australia and died in 2005.

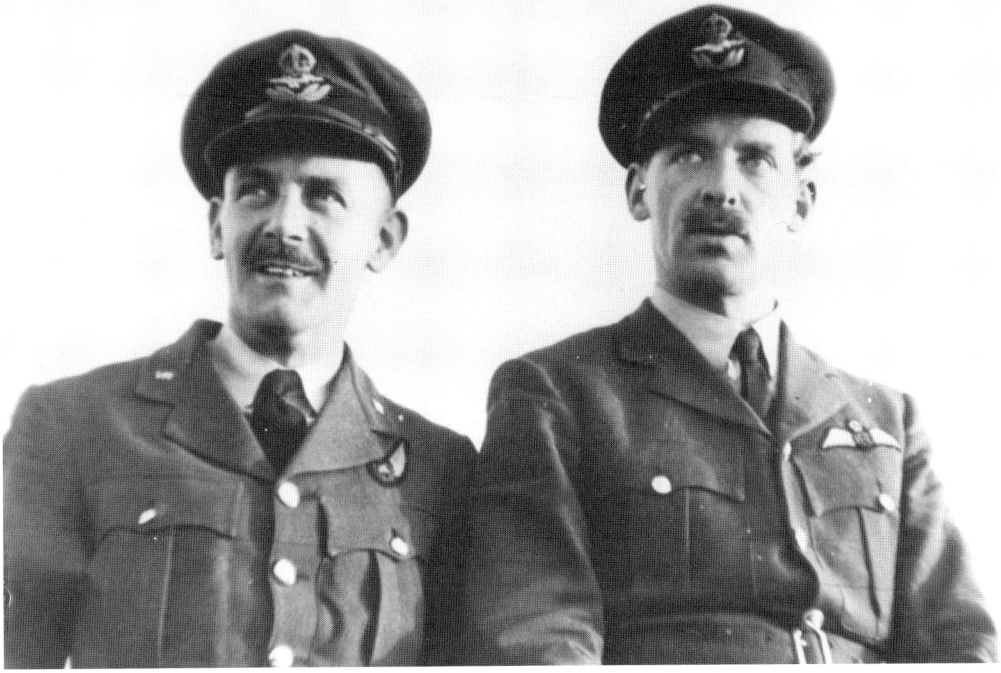

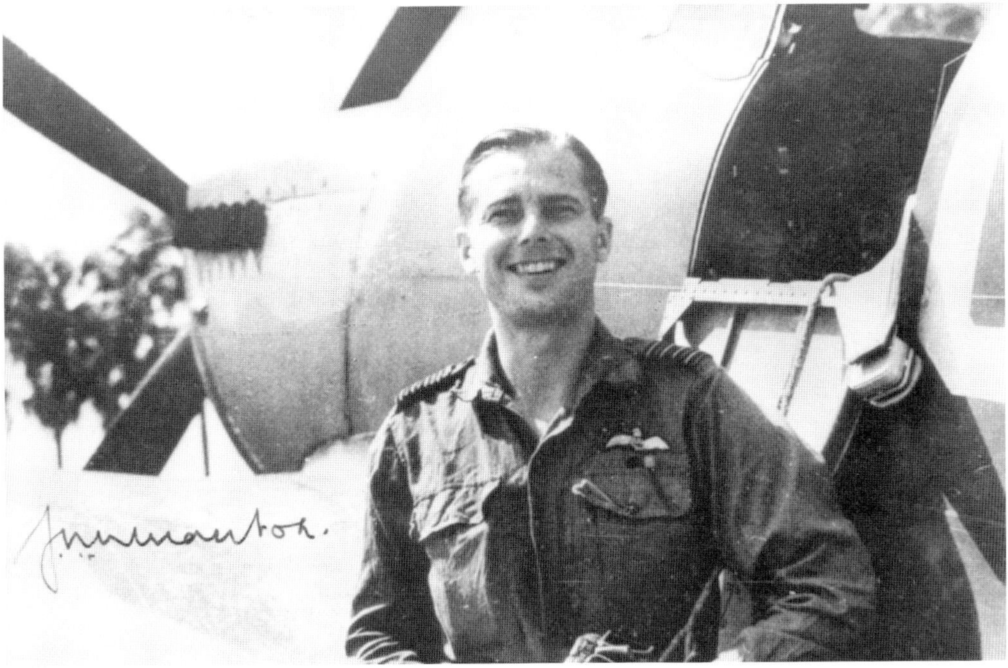

Above: 501 Squadron's Polish Sergeant Anton Glowacki, seen here making out his post-combat report to the unit's intelligence officer, achieved a rare feat in four sorties on 24 August 1940 by destroying five enemy aircraft – thus becoming an ace in one day. His final score was eight destroyed, one shared destroyed, three probables and five damaged. Glowacki survived the war and was an incredibly experienced pilot, having flown 5,800 hours with the Polish Air Force, 2,656 with the RAF, and 648 with the post-war RNZAF in addition to many hours of civilian pleasure flying after retirement in 1975. He died in 1980.

Opposite: Pilot Officer H.L. 'Laurie' Whitbread was a grammar school boy from Ludlow, Shropshire, who took a Short Service Commission in March 1939. During the Dunkirk fighting and Battle of Britain he flew Spitfires with 222 Squadron, and made several combat claims. He was shot down and killed in combat with Me 109s over Kent on 20 September 1940. The author researched Laurie's short life many years ago and most recently told the story in *Spitfire Voices* (2010).

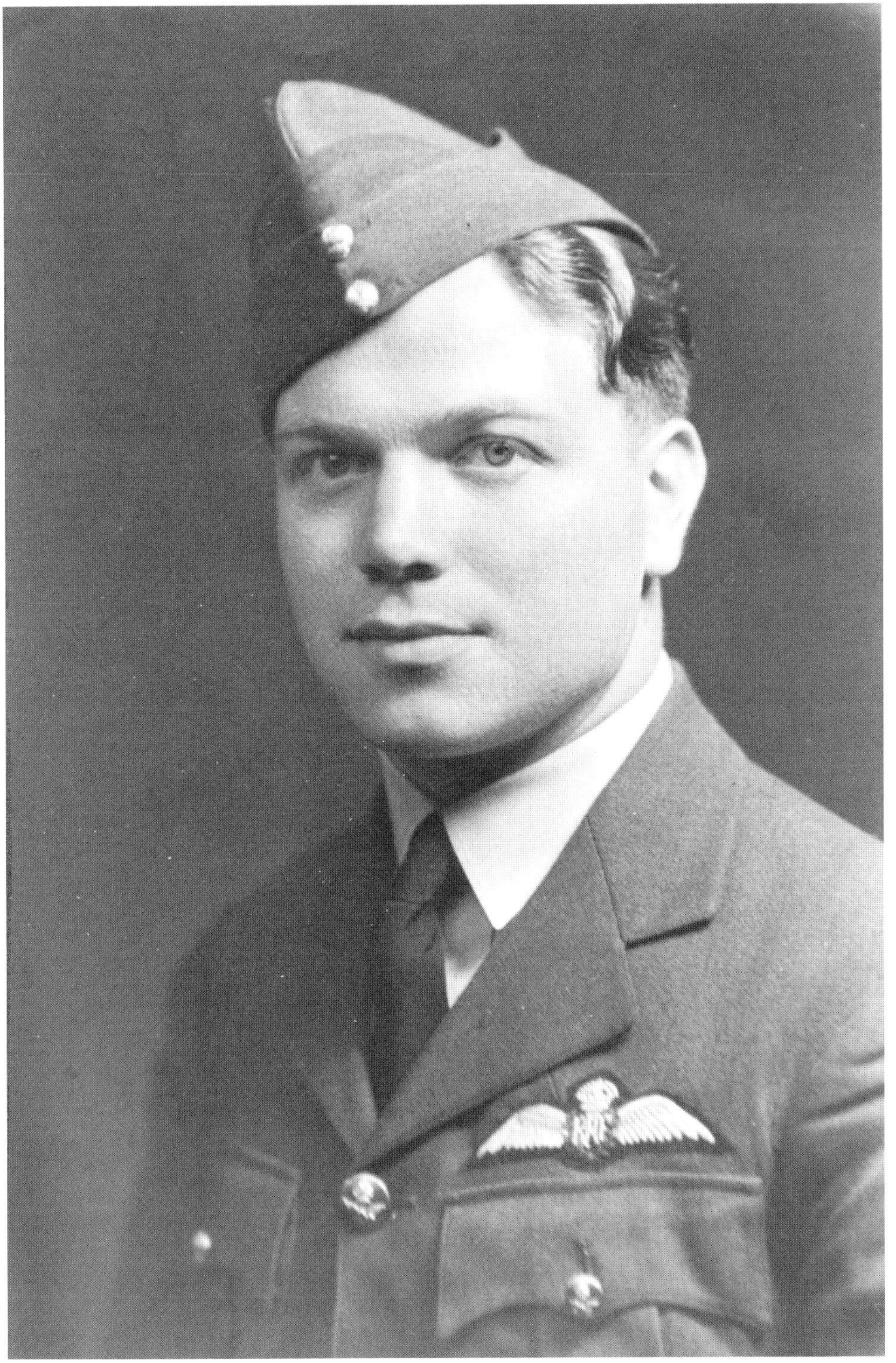

Above: Sergeant-pilots – all reservists – passing the time during training at Montrose. At extreme left is Charlton 'Wag' Haw, who was later part of the RAF deployment to Russia in 1941, and second right is Denis Helcke. Both flew Hurricanes with 504 Squadron during the Battle of Britain, during which Helcke lost his life. Haw became a decorated ace, survived the war and died in 1993.

Opposite above: Pilots of 504 Squadron at Filton during the Battle of Britain. From left: unknown; Pilot Officer Trevor Parsons (killed in a flying accident 1942); Squadron Leader John Sample DFC (killed in a flying accident, 1941); Flight Lieutenant Michael Rook (killed in a flying accident 1948); Flying Officer Blair White (missing in action, 1943) – and the only survivor, Sergeant Charlton 'Wag' Haw, who died in 1993.

Opposite below: Another 504 Squadron group at Filton: from left: Pilot Officer Trevor Parsons, Flying Officer Blair White, Sergeant Charlton Haw, and an unknown sergeant, possibly not aircrew. They are examining the Squadron's battle trophies, souvenirs from German aircraft 504 had destroyed over the West Country on 27 September 1940.

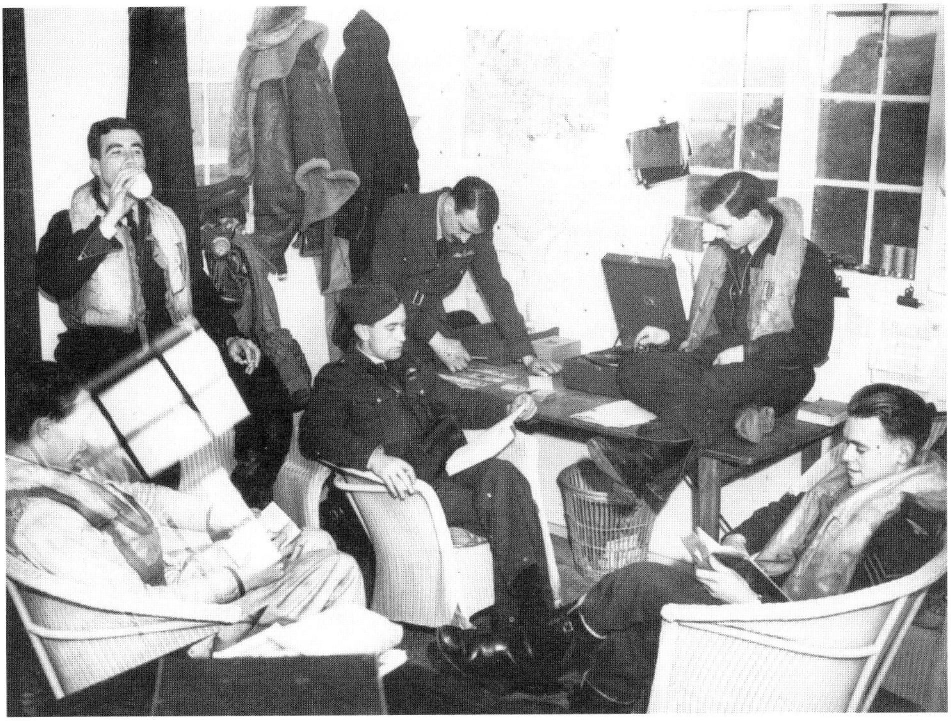

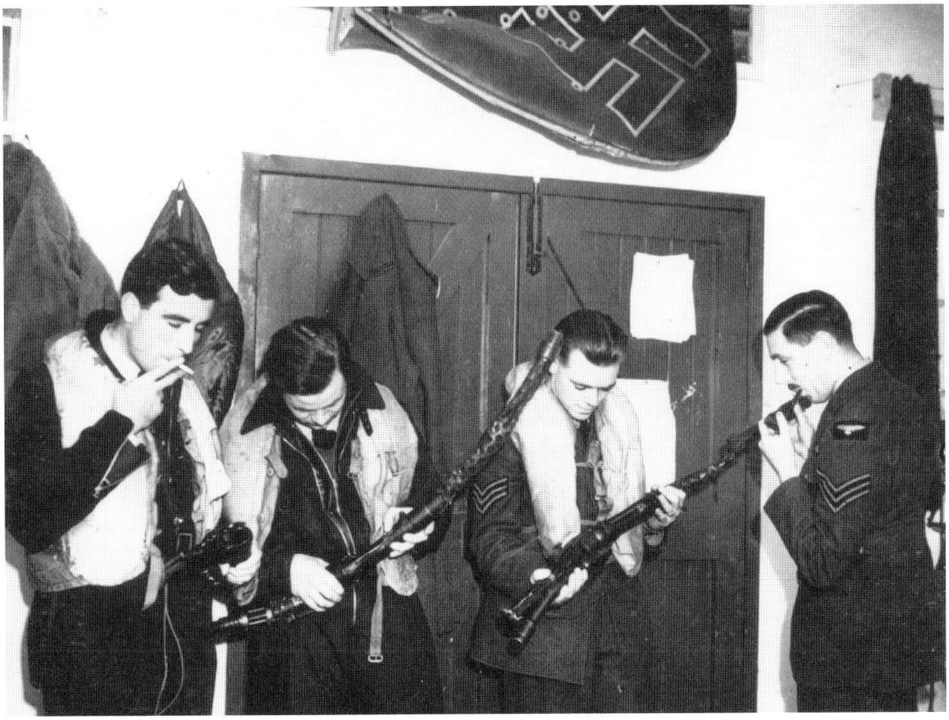

Above: Pilot Officer Tony Parsons (left) and Flight Lieutenant Michael Rook on readiness at Filton and outside the 504 Squadron pilots' hut. The chalk board indicates pilots' availability.

Opposite above: A line-up of 501 Squadron Hurricane pilots at readiness, Kenley, September 1940; from left: Sergeant T.G. Pickering, Flying Officer D.A.E. Jones, Flying Officer V.R. Snell, Sergeant S.A.H. Whitehouse, unidentified, Sergeant J.J.K. Gent, Flight Sergeant P.F. Morfill, next two unidentified, Pilot Officer R.C. Dafforn and the Polish Pilot Officer S. Witorzenc.

Opposite below: An excellent snapshot of 501 Squadron Hurricane pilots at readiness, this time at Gravesend in August 1940; from left: Sergeant T.G. Pickering, Sergeant R.J.K. Gent, Flight Sergeant Peter Morfill, Sergeants P.C.P. Farnes, and A. Glowacki (Polish), unidentified, Sergeants W.B. Henn, S.A.H. Whitehouse and J.H. Lacey, and Pilot Officer R.C. Dafforn.

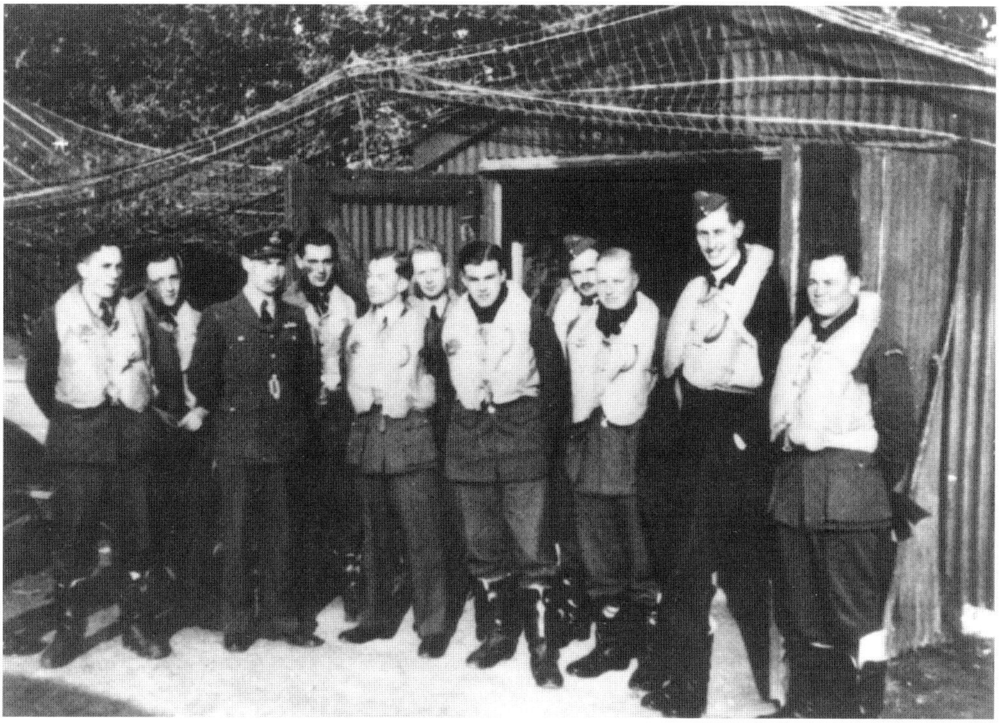

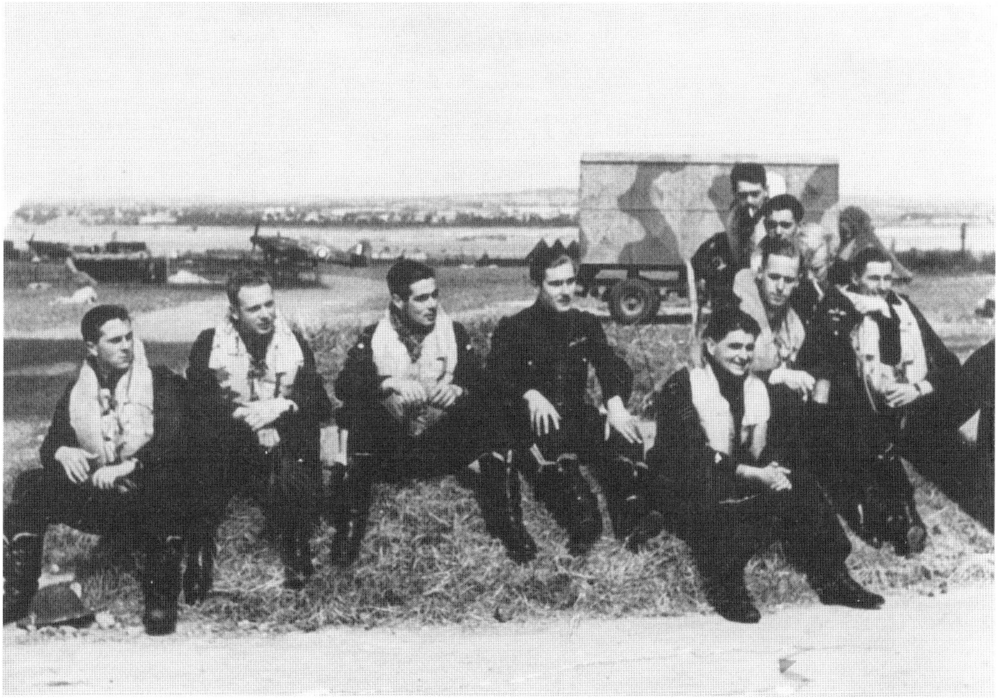

Left: John Gibson was a New Zealander who took a Short Service Commission in 1938. He joined 501 Squadron in France on 21 May 1940, opening his account a few days later. During an extensive operational career at home and overseas, his final score was twelve and one shared, two unconfirmed destroyed, one possible and another damaged; he received the DFC and survived the war; he died in July 2000.

Opposite above: Pilot Officer W.P.H. 'Robin' Rafter, a replacement pilot shot down on his first operational flight with 603 Squadron at Hornchurch, on 5 September 1940, and thrown clear of his Spitfire when the Sutton harness snapped. Whilst descending by parachute he was 'buzzed' by an Me 109 and feared he would be shot – but the German was driven off and shot down by Pilot Officer Basil 'Stapme' Stapleton; the enemy pilot, who was captured, was none other than the infamous Franz von Werra, 'The One That Got Away'. Hospitalised with a head injury from having been catapulted through his Spitfire's Perspex canopy, he returned to 603 Squadron but was killed on his first patrol, on 29 November 1940, when his aircraft fell out of formation and dived into the ground – oxygen system failure being the possible cause. His brother, Pilot Officer Charles Rafter, was a Wellington pilot killed the previous month in a landing accident at Stradishall (214 Squadron); the brothers were the sons of Sir Charles Rafter, Birmingham's Chief Constable. They are buried together in the city, at St Peter's, Harborne.

Below: Sergeant John Gilders, another reservist, joined 72 Squadron at Acklington in June 1940, surviving a nocturnal crash-landing before going with the Squadron to Biggin Hill at the end of August. The following month he became an ace, and after the Battle of Britain joined 41 Squadron at Hornchurch, where this snapshot was taken shortly before his death on 21 February 1941. On that day, his Spitfire dived into the ground near Chilham, but the pilot's remains were not recovered until 1994, when certain enthusiasts, supported by the Gilders family, contravened the Protection of Military Remains Act, 1986, and excavated the crash site – something that the authorities should have done years before. Long after he died, therefore, Sergeant Gilders was buried at Brookwood Military Cemetery.

155

Above: 'Bowler hatted' pilots of 222 Squadron at Hornchurch during the Battle of Britain – during August 1940 the steel helmets were a necessity, as the Station was heavily bombed.

Opposite above: Some wounded aircrew recuperated at Torquay's Palace Hotel, where this snapshot was taken of a band the patients formed – playing the 'Jew's Harp' is Flight Lieutenant James Brindley Nicolson, whose 'signal act of valour' over Southampton on 16 August 1940 earned him the Victoria Cross; at second right is Pilot Officer William Walker of 616 Squadron, who was shot down and wounded on 26 August 1940.

Opposite below: Pilots of 32 Squadron snapped at readiness by Flight Lieutenant Peter Brothers, Biggin Hill, July 1940; from left: Pilot Officer J.P. Pfeiffer, Flight Lieutenant J.B.W. Humpherson, Flying Officer P.M. Gardner, Squadron Leader Mike Crossley, Flying Officer D.H. Grice, and Pilot Officer J.F. Pain; seated, from left: Pilot Officers A.F. Eckford, and the Polish K. Pniak and B.A. Wlasnowski.

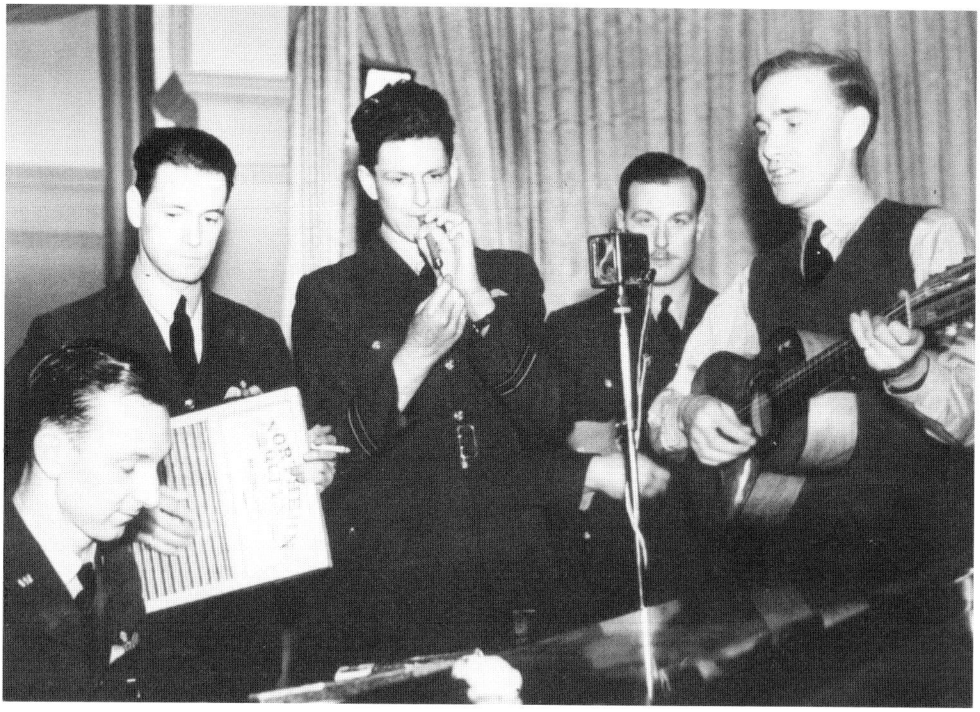

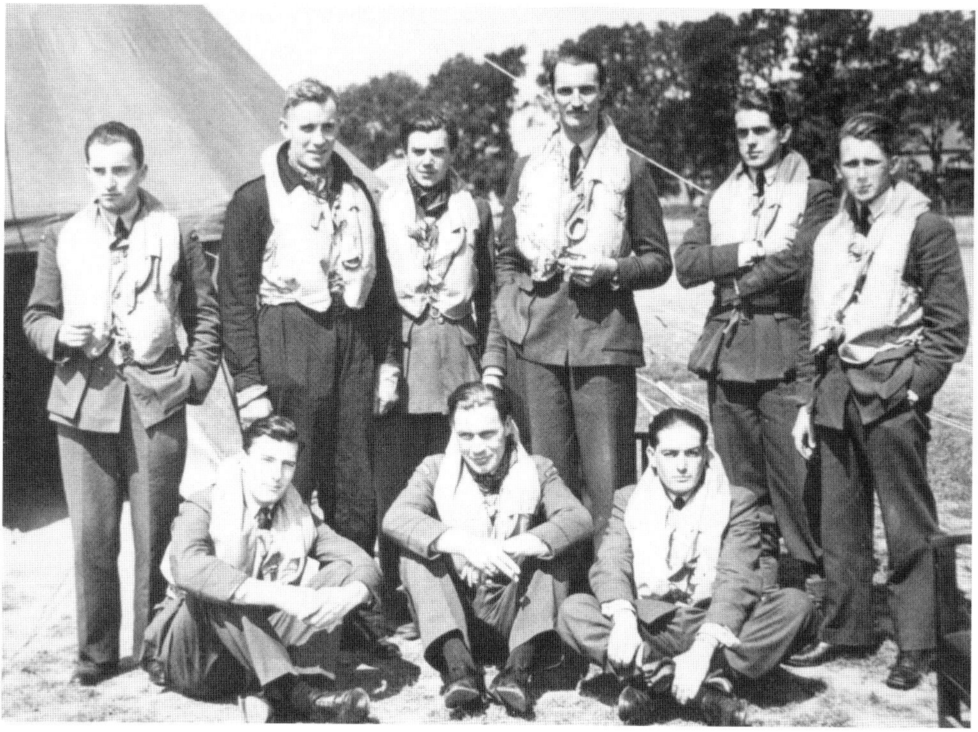

A famous image indeed, of 32 Squadron pilots at readiness, Hawkinge, July 1940; from left: Pilot Officers R.F. Smythe, K.R. Gilman and E. Proctor, Flight Lieutenant P.M. Brothers, Pilot Officers D.H. Grice, P.M. Gardner and A.F. Eckford.

Another image from the same famous sequence, showing the same pilots as in the previous photograph. This is currently in the process of being recreated in bronze, life-size, for the Kent Battle of Britain Museum's 'Spirit of The Few' memorial at Hawkinge.

THE MEN AGAINST GOERING

HULTON'S NATIONAL WEEKLY SHOULD EUROPE STARVE? 3ᴰ

By Rt. Hon. J. R. CLYNES, P.C., M.P.

AUGUST 31, 1940   Vol. 8. No. 9

Pilot Officer Keith Gillman became the face of Fighter Command when appearing on the front cover of the 31 August 1940 edition of *Picture Post* – six days previously he had been shot down over the Channel and reported missing. Never seen again, Pilot Officer Gillman, from Dover, is commemorated on the Runnymede Memorial.

During a combat over the Channel, 32 Squadron's Pilot Officer Rupert Smythe had a lucky escape when a German bullet ripped through the surface of his leather flying helmet – the pilot was unscathed and here shows Flight Lieutenant Brothers, his Flight Commander, the resulting damage.

An oft neglected story is that of the attacks on Britain in 1940 by Mussolini's Corpo Aero Italiano – although this was hardly successful given that the aircraft involved, Fiat BR20 bombers and Fiat CR42 biplane fighters were not of the standard required for daylight operations over England. It was not, however, until 24 October 1940 that the Italians first attacked, ineffectively bombing Harwich that night. Their first daylight raid targeted Deal five days later, and a fighter sweep on 1 November 1940 went unopposed. These continued for another three weeks, and night attacks on Lowestoft, Ipswich, Harwich and Felixstowe only ceased in February 1941, when the Italian air contingent returned to Italy. On 11 November 1940, some fifty Italian aircraft attacked a convoy off Lowestoft – but were intercepted by the Hurricanes of 46 and 257 Squadrons – three CR42s and three BR20s were destroyed, with at least ten more damaged. In this photograph, Squadron Leader Bob Stanford Tuck (centre), commander of 257 Squadron, based at North Weald (who was not flying himself that day) poses for the press with some of his pilots – including the Canadian Flight Lieutenant Peter 'Cowboy' Blatchford (left, kneeling), who claimed several Italians that day, and the Polish Pilot Officer Karel Pniak, wearing an Italian *elmetto*, who shared the destruction of a CR42 with Pilot Officer John Kay (second left). The engagement was forever known by Tuck's men as 'The Chianti Party'.

Above: Eric Lock, a farmer's son from Shropshire, was an exceptional shot, having learned to shoot game on the wing at an early age. A reservist, he achieved considerable success flying Spitfires with 41 Squadron from Hornchurch in September 1940, receiving the DFC. On 17 November 1940, however, he was shot-up by a 109 and crash-landed at Martlesham Heath. Such were his wounds that he was admitted to the Royal Victoria Hospital, East Grinstead, and became a founder member of the Guinea Pig Club, for aircrew treated by the plastic surgeon Sir Archibald McIndoe. Whilst in hospital Lock was appointed to the DSO, and resumed operational flying in July 1941. His successes continued whilst serving as a flight commander on 611 Squadron the following year, but his luck ran out on 3 August 1941, when reported missing after a low-level nuisance raid on targets of opportunity near Calais. The full story is told in the author's *Spitfire Down* (2022). Like Peter Brown in photograph 29, Lock is wearing a highly prized captured German *schwimmveste*.

Opposite above: Pilot Officer Ian Muirhead (left) and Pilot Officer Charles English (right), both of 605 Squadron, enjoying a pint with an unknown friend. English was killed in action over Kent on 7 October 1940, as was Muirhead eight days later. The latter had received a DFC on 28 June 1940, which was the first decoration awarded to 605, a Hurricane squadron heavily engaged during the Battle of Britain, losing eight pilots.

Right: Pilot Officer Dudley
Stewart-Clark was a wealthy
Scottish Etonian, snapped here
at Edinburgh races. A volunteer
reservist and member of the
auxiliary 603 Squadron, he went
to Hornchurch with the Squadron
and made several combat claims
before being shot down off
Margate on 3 September 1940,
by Hauptmann Erich Bode of II/
JG 26. Dudley baled out of his
Spitfire, wounded in the leg. He
survived, but was shot down
again, on 21 June 1941, crash-
landing on the Goodwin Sands,
from which he was fortunately
rescued. Sadly, on 19 September
1941, he was killed in action
over France whilst serving
as a flight commander on
72 Squadron.

Above: James Caistor was a pre-war airman selected for pilot training, who joined 603 Squadron at Turnhouse in October 1939, when a sergeant-pilot, having already flown in Palestine before the war. He saw a surprising amount of action with German reconnaissance bombers off Scotland whilst with 603 Squadron at Turnhouse, and went to Hornchurch with the Squadron, where further successes followed. He was commissioned in August 1940, but on 6 September 1940 was shot down over the Channel, making a forced-landing in France, and being captured; he was awarded the DFM a week later. His Spitfire, X4260, was one of two captured in such circumstances in the Battle of Britain, during which Pilot Officer Caistor became one of only several RAF fighter pilots to become prisoners – he is seen here being taken into captivity. He died in 1994.

Opposite above: 222 Squadron, Hornchurch in September 1940. Pilot Officer John Broadhurst changes a bulb, watched by Sergeant Reg Johnson. The former was killed in action on 7 October 1940 and is buried at Hornchurch Cemetery. Reg Johnson survived the war but died literally immediately after writing his Battle of Britain recollections for the author – featured in *Letters From The Few* (2020).

Opposite below: From the album of Air Marshal Sir Denis Crowley-Milling, who is pictured second left whilst a volunteer reservist learning to fly at Derby in 1937. At extreme left is Alan Feary, who would be killed in action flying Spitfires with 609 Squadron on 7 October 1940.

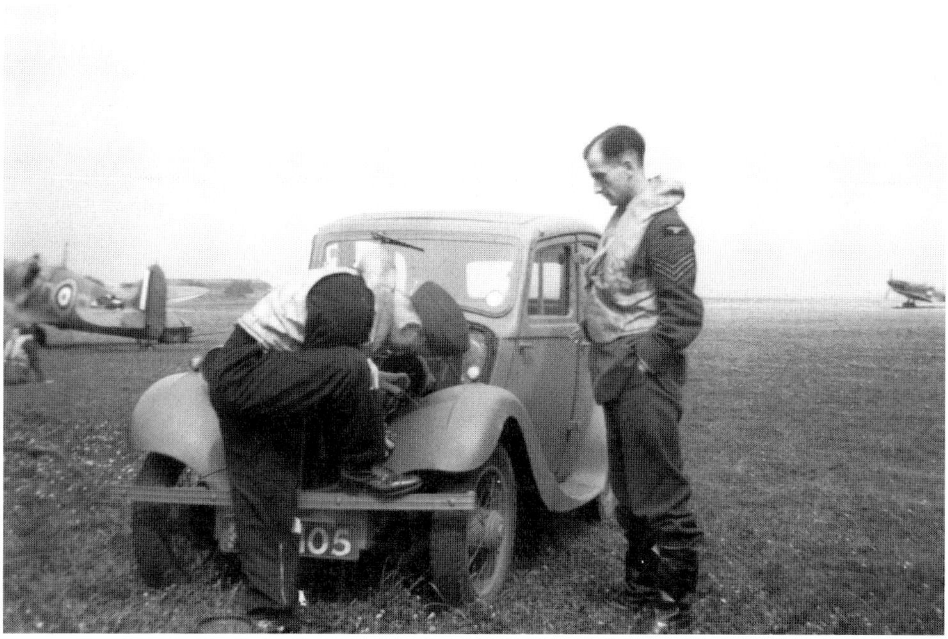
105

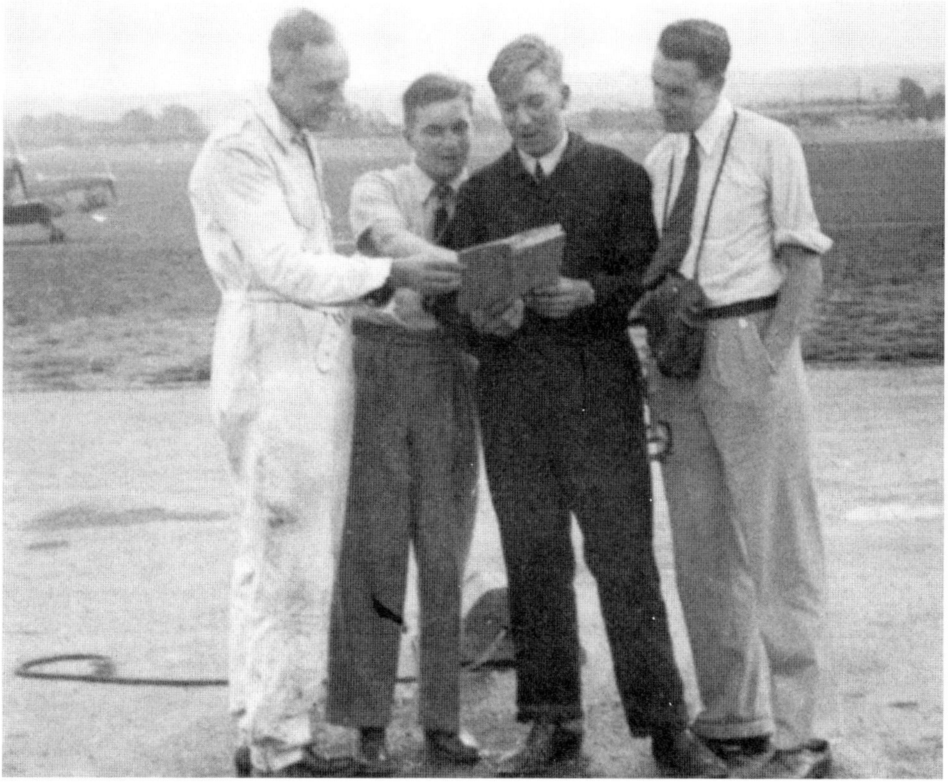

Above: Pilot Officer Dudley Williams (left) and Flying Officer Eric 'Boy' Marrs DFC (see photograph 140) of 152 Squadron at readiness, Warmwell, August 1940; the Irvin-jacketed officer is unidentified but not believed to have been a pilot. Williams became a successful fighter pilot awarded the DFC, and survived the war; he died in 1976.

Opposite: Olympian Squadron Leader Don Finlay DFC, commander of 41 Squadron, steadying the celebratory cake being cut by Flight Lieutenant Norman Ryder DFC on the occasion of the unit's 100th kill. Rear row, from left: Sergeants Robert Angus and Terry Healey; middle: Squadron Leader Finlay, Flying Officer Dennis Adams and Sergeant John Gilders; front row: Flight Lieutenant Ryder, Pilot Officer Roy Ford, Pilot Officer Fred Aldridge.

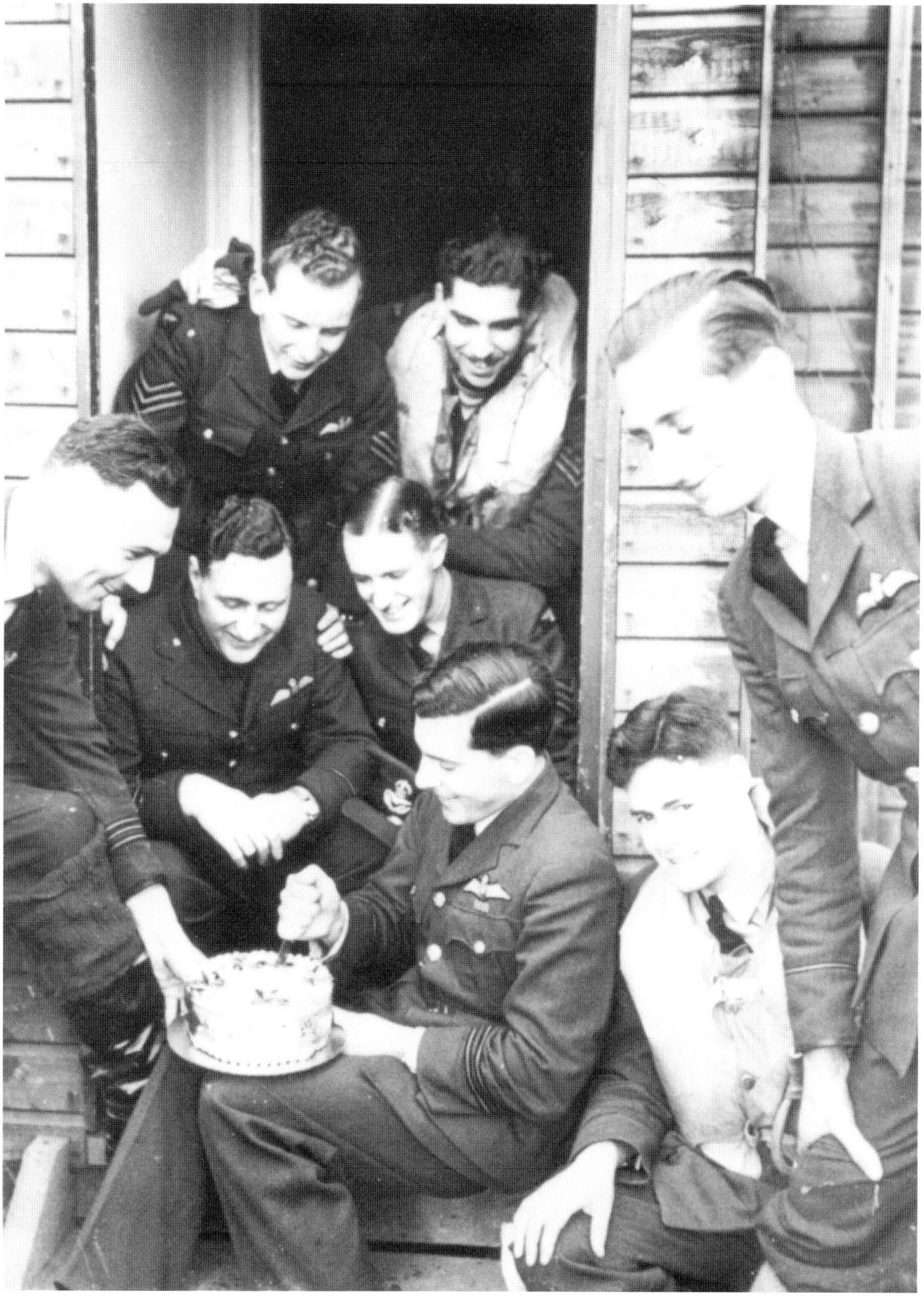

Richard Demetriadi, son of Sir Stephen, a wealthy businessman, whose sister, Amalia, married 'The Flying Etonian', namely son of the first air VC, Flight Lieutenant William Rhodes-Moorhouse, who enjoyed an incredibly privileged lifestyle. The older 'Willie' joined the socially elite 601 Squadron of the Auxiliary Air Force, known as the 'Millionaires' Mob', and arranged membership of this exclusive unit for his brother-in-law – pictured here whilst flying Blenheims before the unit converted to Hurricanes. On 11 August 1940, 601 Squadron was based at Tangmere and embroiled in a great aerial battle over a convoy off Portland, from which Flying Officer Demetriadi failed to return. It fell to Willie to break the news to his family at Ditchling, Sussex.

Above: On 3 September 1940, Flight Lieutenant Rhodes-Moorhouse was invested with the DFC at Buckingham Palace by King George VI, and is pictured here after that occasion with his beautiful wife, Amalia, and mother, Linda (also a keen civilian pilot). Three days later, Willie was shot down and killed over Kent. This tragic and deeply moving story is told in full in the author's *Battle of Britain 1940: The Finest Hour's Human Cost* (2020).

Right: Pilot Officer Philip 'Pip' Cardell was also a volunteer reservist mobilised when war broke out, and during the Battle of Britain flew Spitfires with 603 Squadron at Hornchurch. Having damaged a He 111 earlier in the month, on 27 September 1940 'Pip' was shot-up off Folkestone but was forced to bale out when his aircraft became uncontrollable. Jumping at 500 feet, his parachute failed but his friend, the South African Flying Officer Peter Dexter, landed on the nearby beach and went out with locals to retrieve the downed pilot who, sadly, was found to be dead. He was buried in his home village at Great Paxton, Huntingdonshire, and, again, this story is told, in detail, in *Battle of Britain 1940: The Finest Hour's Human Cost* (2020).

Left: Flying Officer Peter Dexter, who so gallantly went to 'Pip' Cardell's assistance, was a successful pilot and had a narrow escape himself during the Battle of Britain, on 2 October 1940, when he was shot down and wounded, only just managing to escape his aircraft whilst high enough to deploy his parachute. His luck ran out, though, on 14 July 1941, when he collided with another Spitfire over France whilst serving with 611 Squadron, and was killed. He is buried at Samer Communal Cemetery.

Below: Squadron Leader Rupert 'Lucky' Leigh (third from right), the commander of 66 Squadron, with some of his pilots at Gravesend, September 1940; from left: the Canadian Pilot Officer Hugh Reilley, Pilot Officer 'Bogle' Bodie, Flight Lieutenant George Christie, the South African Pilot Officer Arthur Watkinson, Flight Lieutenant Robert 'Bobby' Oxspring, and Pilot Officer Hubert 'Dizzy' Allen. 66 'Clickety-Click' Squadron was heavily engaged during the summer and autumn of 1940, flying from both Kenley and Gravesend.

A true forgotten hero: Wing Commander H.F. 'Billy' Burton DSO DFC CdeG. A Cranwellian, in 1936 Billy won the coveted Sword of Honour and was undoubtedly destined for air rank. At the time of Dunkirk he was a flight commander on 66 Squadron, and saw action, after which he was promoted to command and re-build 616 Squadron, which had been decimated operating from Kenley. This he did, and the Squadron was soon contributing to Douglas Bader's Duxford Wing operations. In February 1941, Billy took the Squadron south, to Tangmere. The following month Wing Commander Bader arrived to be the Station's first Wing Leader, after which 616 Squadron was heavily engaged over France throughout the 'season'. Awarded the DSO, Billy next saw action leading a P-40-equipped wing in the western desert. Tragically, after Rommel had been beaten in North Africa, Billy and other officers were returning from home leave when shot down in their unarmed Hudson over the Bay of Biscay on 3 June 1943 – all involved, including another Battle of Britain ace, Squadron Leader Osgood 'Pedro' Hanbury, were killed. It was a tragic loss and great blow to the Desert Air Force. Billy's story is told in full, for the first time, in the author's *Forgotten Heroes of the Battle of Britain*.

171

Squadron Leader Harold Starr was a pre-war Short Service Commissioned officer and army cooperation pilot who converted to Hurricanes in July 1940. Given command of 253 Squadron at Turnhouse, he took the Squadron to Kenley on 29 August 1940 – and two days later was shot down and killed. His brother, Wing Commander N.J. Starr DFC, was also killed during the war.

Above: Sergeant Cyril Babbage, a Spitfire pilot of 602 Squadron, being brought ashore at Bognor Regis, Sussex, having been shot down over the Channel by Hauptmann Hans-Karl Mayer of 1/JG 53 on 26 August 1940. Babbage was another successful RAFVR fighter pilot and was awarded the DFM on 25 October 1940. He later flew with the Tangmere Wing in 1941, destroying an early Fw 190, and survived a tour on Mosquitos. Having remained in the post-war service, he retired to Herefordshire and died in 1977.

Right: Sergeant James 'Morris' Cowley joined the RAF in 1931 and was another Halton apprentice who became a fighter pilot. During the Battle of Britain he flew Hurricanes with 87 Squadron, based at Exeter, destroying a Me 110 over Portland on 15 August 1940. He was wounded that day, however, when shot-up and injured in a heavy forced-landing. He never flew operationally again, and nothing more of him is known after leaving the service as a flight lieutenant in 1946.

Sergeants Cowley and Thorogood pictured at Bibury with Flying Officer Rod Rayner, all of 87 Squadron. Rayner fought well in the Battles of France and Britain, destroying a number of enemy aircraft and awarded the DFC. After the Battle of Britain, still flying Hurricanes, 87 Squadron went over to the night-fighter role, and on the night of 10 April 1941, Rayner, by then commanding 'A' Flight, caught and damaged a He 111 on the 'Brum' run over Gloucester and Tewkesbury. He survived the war and died in 1982.

The diminutive Flight Lieutenant 'Widge' Gleed (centre) and his pilots of 87 Squadron's 'A' Flight at the famous Swan Hotel, Bibury, Gloucestershire, in August 1940; from left: Flying Officer Rafael Watson, the New Zealander Pilot Officer Ken Tait, 'Widge', Flying Officer Roddy Rayner, and Pilot Officer Peter Comely – reported missing off Portland on 15 August 1940, and who has no known grave. Only Watson and Rayner survived the war.

Above: Pilot Officer Frantisek Dolezal was a Czechoslovak pilot flying Spitfires with 19 Squadron at Fowlmere. An experienced pre-war airman, Dolezal scored aerial victories flying with the l'Armee de l'Air during the Fall of France, before making his way to England and continuing the fight. Another successful fighter pilot awarded both the DSO and DFC, he survived the war only to be killed in a flying accident when a passenger in a Su204 aircraft over Moravia on 4 October 1945.

Opposite: Another of 19 Squadron's Czechoslovak pilots was Sergeant Frantisek Marek – killed on 14 September 1940 when his Spitfire crashed near Orsett owing to oxygen failure, he was buried at Eastbrookend Cemetery, Barking, Essex. More recently artefacts from his Spitfire have appeared for sale on a popular online auction site for absurdly high prices.

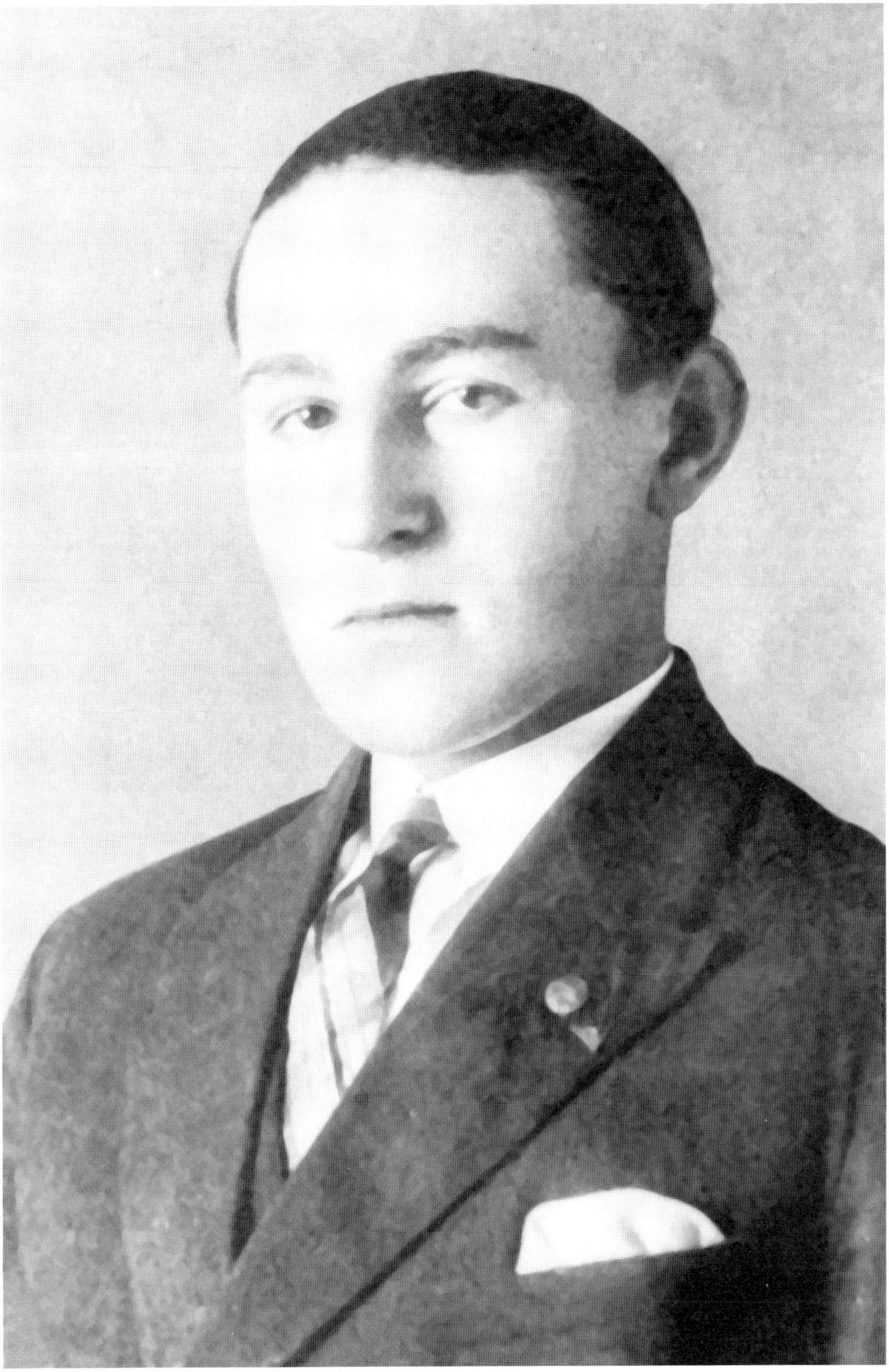

Above: Flight Lieutenant Colin MacFie, from Cheltenham, first saw action with 611 Squadron before becoming a flight commander on Billy Burton's 616 Squadron. He made a number of combat claims and received the DFC, but was shot down over France and captured on 5 July 1941. After repatriating he remained in the RAF until 1963, retiring to Scotland, and died in 1982.

Opposite above: Flight Lieutenant Derek 'Bottle' Boitel-Gill commanded 'A' Flight of 152 Squadron at Warmwell during the Battle of Britain, where he is pictured here. Another ace awarded the DFC, he was ultimately killed in a flying accident on 18 September 1941, whilst a wing commander on a training unit.

Opposite below: Pilot Officer Franek Surma was a pre-war Polish Air Force pilot and amongst the first Poles to arrive in Britain. During the summer and autumn of 1940 he served with various RAF fighter squadrons and is pictured here at readiness whilst flying Hurricanes with 607 Squadron at Tangmere in September 1940.

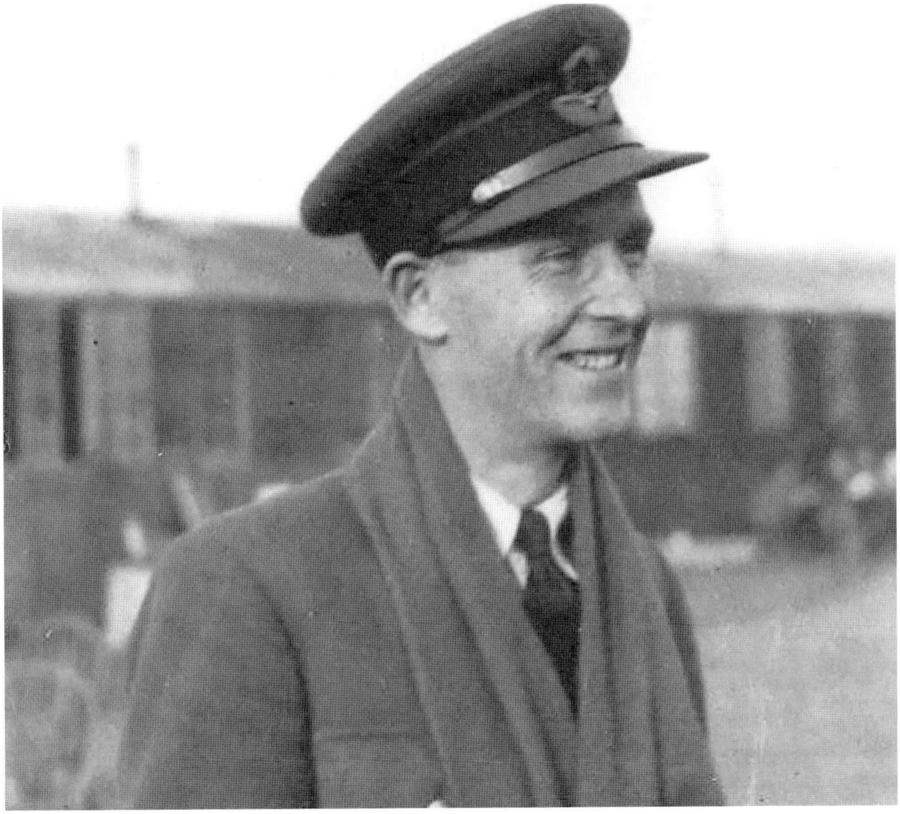

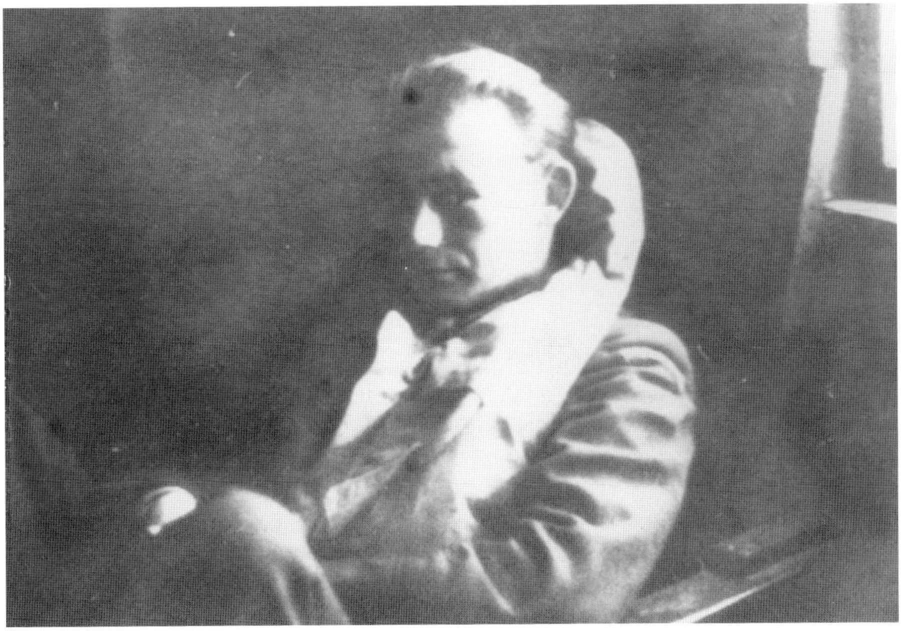

Above: Whilst at Tangmere with 607 Squadron, Pilot Officer Surma flew in Flight Lieutenant Charles 'Chatty' Bowen's Flight. Here, his Flight Commander, sporting a highly prized German schwimmvest, is teaching the Pole to play 'pax'. On 1 October 1940, Bowen was reported missing after a sharp scrap with Me 110s over the Isle of Wight. Surma became an ace, but was also shot down into the sea and reported missing, on 8 November 1941. Neither pilot was ever seen again.

Opposite: Another unsung hero was Richard Edgar Peter Brooker, a pre-war pilot with 56 Squadron at North Weald. During the Battle of Britain he made a number of combat claims, survived being shot-up and wounded, and became a flight commander. In April 1941 he was given command of 1 Squadron, and on the night of 10/11 May 1941, destroyed a He 111 over London. Having received the DFC, Squadron Leader Brooker was posted to the Far East, where he destroyed several Japanese aircraft and was awarded a Bar to the DFC. Back home, promoted to wing commander, Brooker led the Typhoon-equipped 123 Wing and was appointed to the DSO. Sadly, on 16 April 1945, whilst leading 122 Wing at Volkel, Brooker was shot down and reported missing. He is commemorated on the Runnymede Memorial (Malcolm Sutherland).

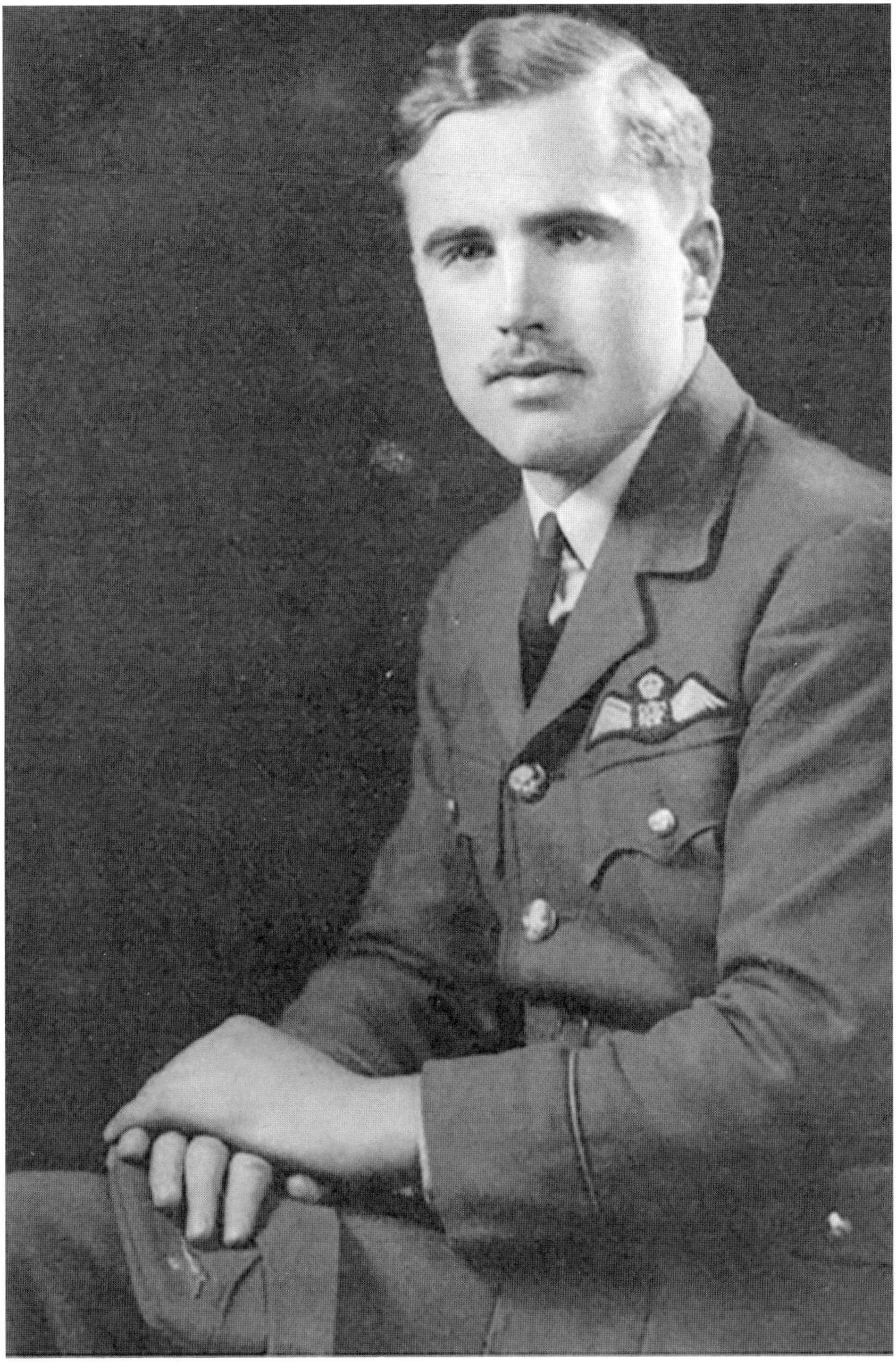

Above: A still from a well-known wartime newsreel short filmed at North Weald during the Battle of Britain, showing, from left, Flight Lieutenant Percy 'Squeak' Weaver, Squadron Leader Graham 'Minnie' Manton, and Flight Lieutenant Richard Brooker; only Manton survived the war.

Left: Geoffrey Matheson first flew with 41 Squadron in 1937 before joining 19 Squadron at Duxford in 1939, flying Spitfires. By June 1940, he was commanding 'A' Flight of 222 Squadron, destroying an Me 109 on 30 August 1940, the Squadron's first at Hornchurch, on which day he was shot down himself and crash-landed near Sittingbourne Paper Mills. The pilot rapidly vacated the aircraft, Spitfire P9443, which then exploded. Fortunately Matheson escaped with minor injuries. He later flew Mosquitos whilst commanding 418 Squadron at Ford, but was reported missing on 24 August 1943.

Flight Lieutenant Matheson and two soldiers with the remains of the Spitfire in which he was shot down on 30 August 1940 and crash-landed near Kemsley Paper Mill, Sittingbourne – fortunately the pilot escaped serious injury when the aircraft exploded.

Flight Lieutenant Matheson and soldiers are joined by a police officer in this snapshot.

Above: The remains of Flight Lieutenant Matheson's cockpit after the explosion.

Opposite above: Flight Lieutenant Matheson and friends after his lucky escape.

Opposite below: Reg Nutter from Dover, was a pre-war volunteer reservist who flew Hurricanes with 257 Squadron at North Weald throughout the Battle of Britain, probably destroyed a Me 109 on 2 September 1940, and survived being shot-up and wounded the following day. He later served as an instructor in Canada before returning to operations, flying Typhoons in Holland. Awarded the DFC, he left the service in 1946 and emigrated to Canada, where he died on 9 December 2014. His story is told in the author's *Letters From The Few* (2020).

To DILIP
KEEP UP
THE GOOD
WORK
R. C. Nutter
AUGUST
1988

From Reg Nutter's album, a snapshot taken at North Weald of 257 Squadron's Flying Officer The Hon David Coke, son of the Earl of Leicester and both an Etonian and former Cambridge scholar. On 12 August 1940, Coke was shot-up over Portsmouth and wounded, as a result of which a finger on his right hand was amputated. He was later shot down and killed over the western desert on 9 December 1941.

Another of Reg Nutter's North Weald snaps, this is 257 Squadron's Flight Lieutenant Howard 'Cowboy' Blatchford DFC, an ace ultimately reported missing in action whilst leading the Coltishall Wing on 3 May 1943.

Above: Pilots of 1 Squadron at Northolt during the Battle of Britain. Fourth from right is Pilot Officer Pat Hancock, later a long-serving Honorary Secretary of the Battle of Britain Fighter Association, and to his left is Pilot Officer J.F.D. 'Tim' Elkington (see photographs 23 and 24). Second right is a Free Frenchman, Jean Demozay, from Nantes, a highly decorated pilot who survived the war only to be killed in a flying accident on 19 December 1945.

Opposite above: Green Section, of 253 Squadron's 'B' Flight at dispersal, Northolt, in May 1940. The pilot at left wearing a forage cap is Pilot Officer Charles Jeffries, a successful fighter pilot who later fought over Malta, receiving the DFC and two Bars; he survived the war and died in 1985. Standing at right is Pilot Officer Len Murch, who made several combat claims in the Battle of Britain but died of poliomyelitis in 1943. Cross-legged at front is Pilot Officer David Jenkins who was shot down and killed on 30 August 1940 whilst the Squadron was operating from Kenley.

Opposite below: Flying Officer Jerzy Jankiewicz (extreme left) describes a recent aerial exploit to his 303 Squadron commander, Squadron Leader Kellett (second left), at Northolt during the Battle of Britain, Sergeant Stanislaw Karubin (second right), who often flew as Kellett's wingman, and Pilot Officer Franciszek Korniki.

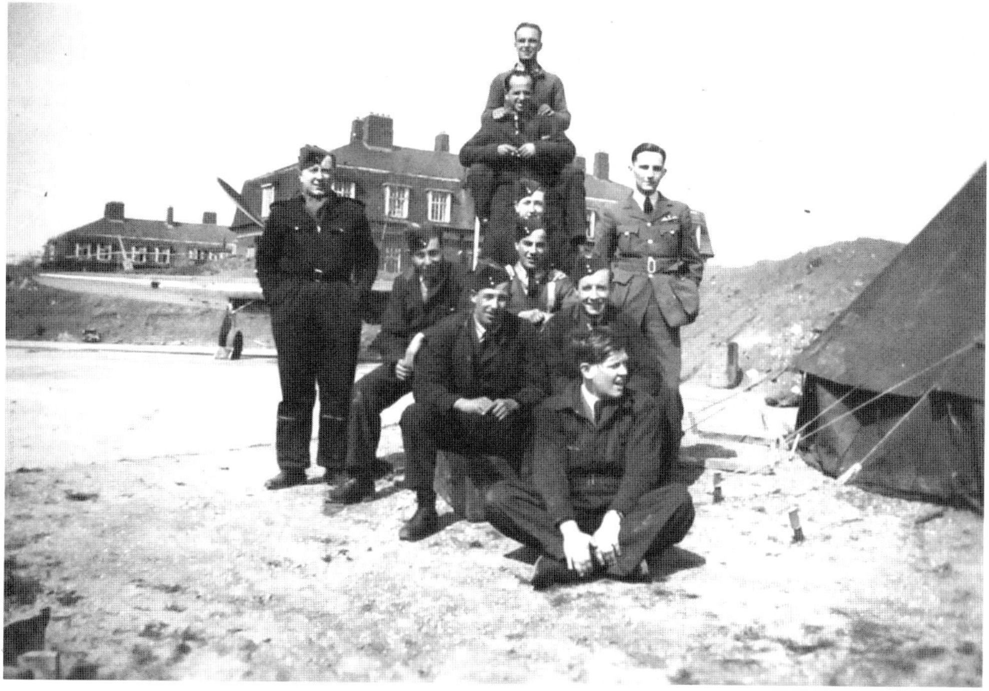

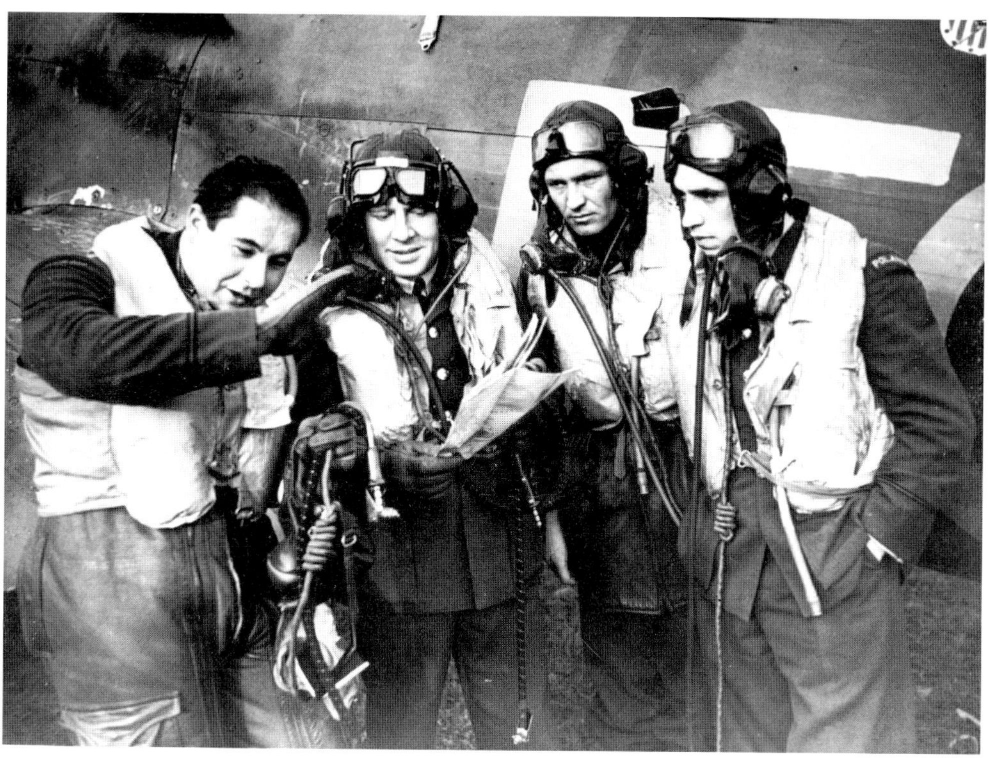

Above: In another posed shot, Squadron Leader Kellett (see photographs 91 and 92), on the Hurricane's wing, along with, from left, Sergeant Karubin, Pilot Officer Kornicki and Flying Officer Jankiewicz.

Left: During the Battle of France, Pilot Officer Peter Parrott appeared on an RAF recruiting poster – he was a successful fighter pilot who flew Hurricanes during the Battle of Britain with both 145 and 605 Squadrons.

Right: Peter Parrott survived the war a wing commander and highly decorated ace who also fought in the Mediterranean campaign. He remained in the RAF until 1967 and died on 27 August 2003. His story is told in the author's *The Final Few* (2015).

Peter L Parrott

Below: Squadron Leader Norman Odbert, briefly commander of 64 Squadron early on during the Battle of Britain, presents his pilots to King George VI at Kenley. Odbert survived the war but his brother, Group Captain Reginald Odbert, was killed flying Wellingtons in 1943. Norman died in August 1999.

Happier times: Flight Lieutenant David Hughes DFC took a Short Service Commission in 1936 and became an army cooperation pilot. Answering Fighter Command's call for volunteers, he converted to Hurricanes and joined 238 Squadron at Middle Wallop as a flight commander on 4 August 1940. Several combat successes followed but he was reported missing on 11 September 1940, after 238 Squadron intercepted German bombers over Kent.

Roy Marples was commissioned in the reserve of RAF officers in 1938 and, at the time of Dunkirk, was flying Spitfires with 616 Squadron. Marples recorded combat successes early on, but was shot down and wounded on 26 August 1940, missing the remainder of the Battle of Britain. Afterwards, he returned to 616 Squadron and received the DFC for his efforts over France the following year, when the Squadron was part of the Tangmere Wing. Having later led 145 Squadron in the western desert, he became a wing leader back home but was killed on 26 April 1944 in a collision with another Spitfire over Sussex.

Above: Policeman's son and grammar school boy Pilot Officer James Edgar 'Johnnie' Johnson was rejected by the socially elite auxiliary air force pre-war and so become a volunteer reservist. He too served in 616 Squadron in 1940 and received the coveted Battle of Britain Clasp, although he saw no action during the summer and autumn of 1940 owing to having an operation on his shoulder. Recovered, Johnnie became a rising star in the Tangmere Wing throughout 1941, and ultimately survived the war as the RAF's officially top-scoring fighter pilot, with 38½ kills, and greatest wing leader. Johnnie eventually retired from the post-war RAF as a highly decorated air vice-marshal; a great friend of the author, the 'AVM' died on 30 January 2001.

Opposite: Having previously been on the reserve, Pilot Officer Jack Hamar took a Short Service Commission and joined 151 Squadron at North Weald in March 1939. Regularly flying as wingman to the squadron's commander, Squadron Leader 'Teddy' Donaldson, Hamar became an ace during the Fall of France and early stage of the Battle of Britain. He was tragically killed in a landing accident at North Weald on 24 July 1940 – on which day his family were at home in Knighton, Radnorshire, celebrating Jack's DFC award when the telegram arrived informing of his death. Jack Hamar's story is told in the author's *Battle of Britain 1940: The Finest Hour's Human Cost* (2020).

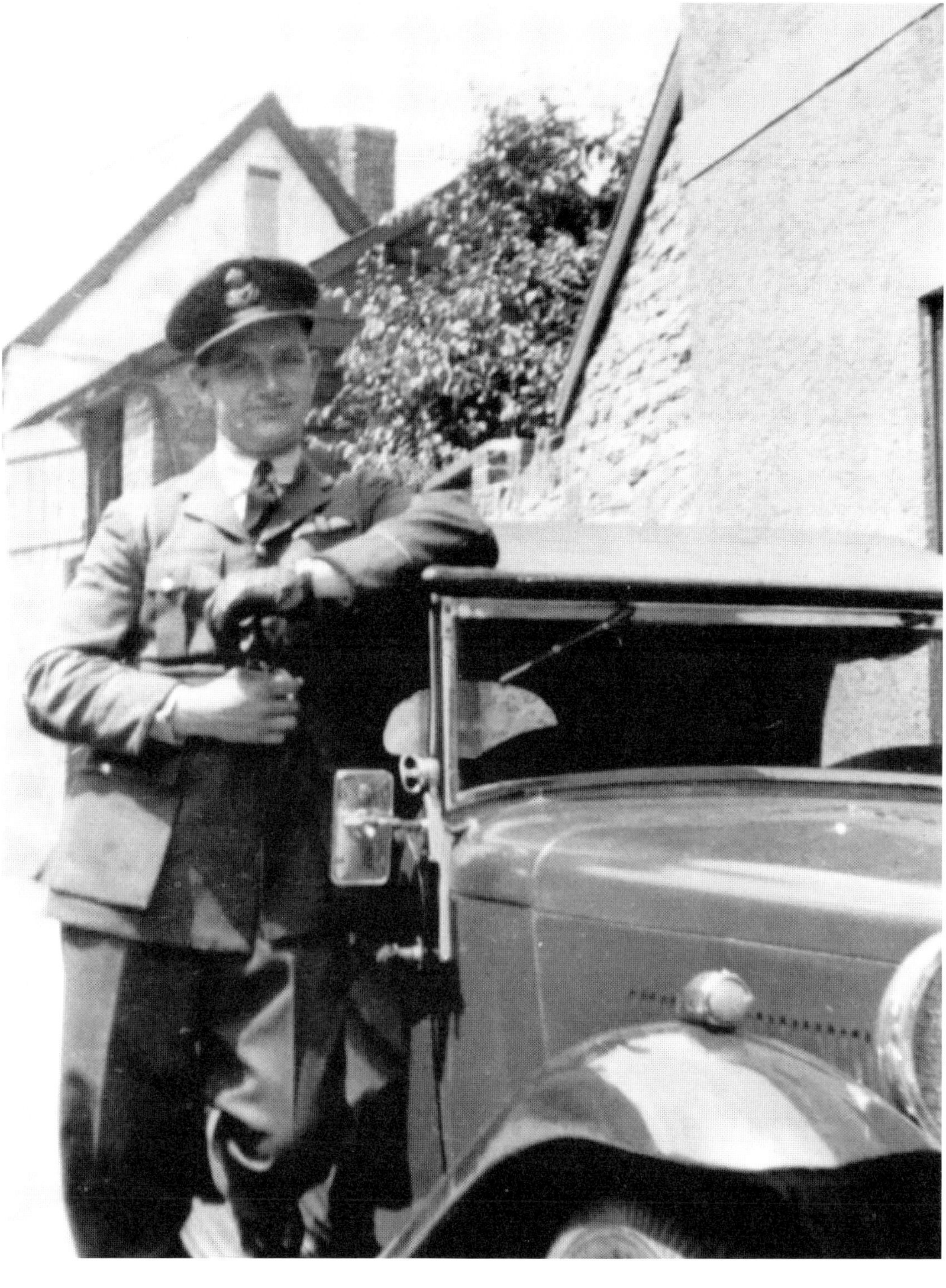

Another Polish pilot embedded in an RAF fighter squadron was Flying Officer Tadeusz Nowierski, who became an ace flying Spitfires with 609 Squadron at Warmwell. He saw extensive operational service during the war as a flight, squadron, and wing commander, in addition to commanding 133 Airfield and a staff college in Kansas. In 1947 he left the service as a highly decorated group captain and returned home to Poland – which was then under Soviet control and behind the 'Iron Curtain'. Like so many returning Poles who had fought in the west, Nowieski was arrested and persecuted by the Stalinist regime, and only able to work as a taxi driver. He died on 2 April 1983.

Above: On 13 August 1940, 609 Squadron destroyed a number of Ju 87 Stukas over Weymouth, and some of the Squadron are snapped here just after that successful engagement. Standing, from left: Pilot Officer Eugene 'Red' Tobin, and American volunteer; the Polish Flying Officer Piotr 'Osti' Ostaszewski-Ostoja, Flying Officer 'Mac' Goodwin, unknown, Pilot Officer Michael Appleby, Flight Lieutenant Frank Howell, Squadron Leader George Darley, Flight Lieutenant James MacArthur, Sergeant Alan Fearey, Flying Officer Tadeusz Nowierski and Flying Officer Charles 'Teeny' Overton; kneeling, from left: Pilot Officers Michael Staples, David Crook and Rogers Miller. In 2021, the author published *The Real Spitfire Pilot*, being the original manuscript of Crook's 1942 memoir *Spitfire Pilot*, and told Miller's story in *Battle of Britain 1940: The Finest Hour's Human Cost* (2020).

Right: Pilot Officer Richard 'Dick' Howley was a Newfoundlander, whose father was a British naval officer serving there before moving his family to Bognor Regis. Dick joined the volunteer reserve in 1938, and joined 141 Squadron at Turnhouse, flying Gloster Gladiators, on 7 October 1939. By 3 June 1940, however, 141 had converted to the Boulton-Paul Defiant turret-fighter and moved to West Malling in Kent on 12 July 1940. A week later, 20-year-old Pilot Officer Howley was shot down and killed over the Channel when 141 Squadron lost nine Defiants to Me 109s of III/JG 51 in what became known as 'The Slaughter of the Innocents'. Still fondly remembered by his sister, Tina Harney, Dick's story is told in the author's *Forgotten Heroes of The Battle of Britain* (2022).

Sergeant Albert Curley was a pre-war airman who qualified as a wireless operator/air-gunner and was crewed with Pilot Officer Dick Howley of 141 Squadron. The pair were flying together when lost over the Channel, when the Defiants of 141 Squadron were massacred by Me 109s. Both airmen remain missing and are commemorated on the Runnymede Memorial.

Pilot Officer Bill Read was a reservist commissioned in June 1940, when he converted to Spitfires. During the Battle of Britain he became a successful fighter pilot flying Spitfires with 603 Squadron at Hornchurch, after which he went out to Russia, flying Hurricanes in the defence of Archangel. Back home he was awarded the AFC and later flew Beaufighters and Mosquitos operationally before serving as a test-pilot. After the war, Bill became a civilian airline pilot until retiring to farm; he died in May 2000.

Tim Vigors was an Etonian and Cranwellian who flew Spitfires with 222 Squadron throughout the Battle of Britain, becoming a decorated ace. He then fought against the Japanese in the Far East, and survived the war. After leaving the service in 1946, after many adventures, he became a leading race horse breeder and owner; he died on 14 November 2003.

Until the Japanese attack on Pearl Harbor on 7 December 1941, the United States was neutral, its strict Neutrality Acts prohibiting American citizens serving in belligerent foreign armed forces. Nonetheless, a surprising number crossed the border into Canada and joined the RCAF before travelling to Britain and being absorbed into the RAF. One such, from Salem, Illinois, was Pilot Officer Phillip 'Uncle Sam' Leckrone, who was commissioned in the RAFVR in August 1940 and converted to Spitfires. He was then posted as a replacement pilot to 616 Squadron on 2 September 1940, after the Squadron had suffered heavy casualties at Kenley, then the following month joined 71 'Eagle' Squadron, the first of three All-American squadrons. Leckrone saw no action in the Battle of Britain but was destined to become 71 Squadron's first fatality, when he was killed as the result of a mid-air collision during a training flight on 5 January 1941. This photograph was amongst those taken by Air Ministry photographer Stanley Devon at RAF Fowlmere on 21 September 1940, when 616 Squadron was contributing to the 12 Group 'Big Wing'.

Left: Stan Turner (right) was a tough Canadian and pre-war officer who flew Hurricanes in Douglas Bader's 242 Squadron at Coltishall and Duxford during the Battle of Britain. Another highly decorated ace, he is pictured here at Brussels-Everé whilst a group captain commanding 127 Airfield. The other officer is Wing Commander Johnnie Johnson, who led 127 Wing in the air. The photograph is from Johnnie's personal album, published by the author as *Spitfire Ace of Aces: The Album* (2021). Turner also survived the war, after which he served in the RCAF until 1965; he died on 23 July 1985.

Opposite above: Another of Johnnie's snapshots shows the great man (left) on the continent in 1944 with another of The Few, Mike Ingle-Finch, who was then commanding 175 (Typhoon) Squadron. A successful pilot with a DFC and Bar, during the Battle of Britain, Mike flew Hurricanes with 56, 151 and 607 Squadron, retiring as a wing commander; he died on 1 February 1992.

Opposite below: After the Battle: three 609 Squadron aces at Buckingham Palace for their DFC investiture after the Battle of Britain; from left: Pilot Officer John Curchin, Flight Lieutenant Frank Howell and Pilot Officer David Crook. Only Howell would survive the war, but was killed at Odiham on 9 May 1948 when struck by a Vampire jet whilst recording the aircraft landing on cine film.

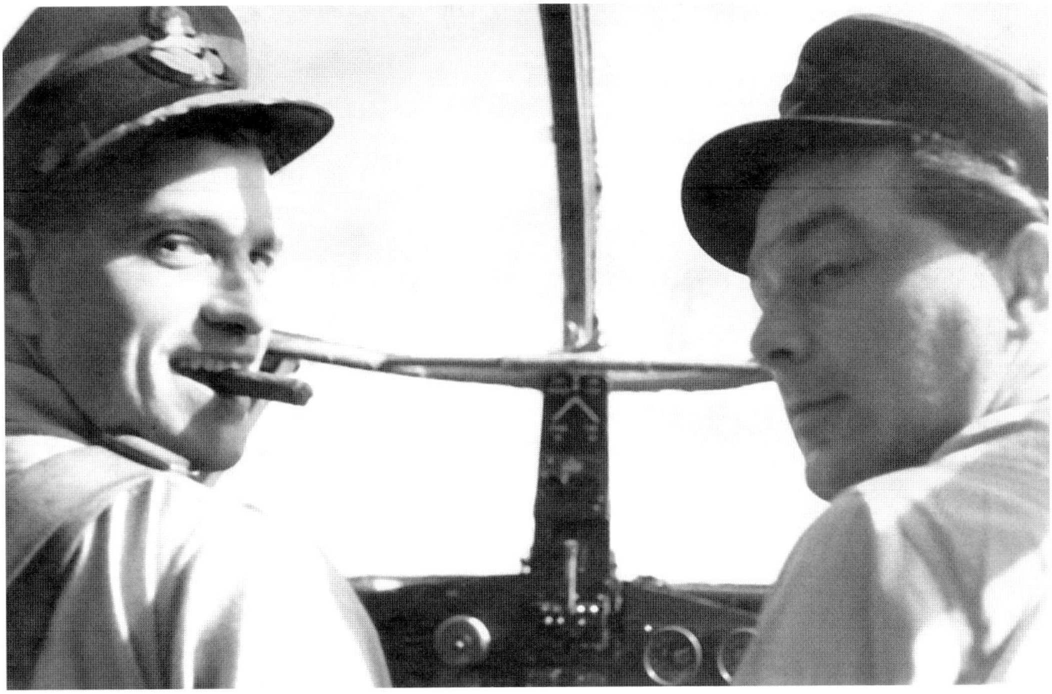

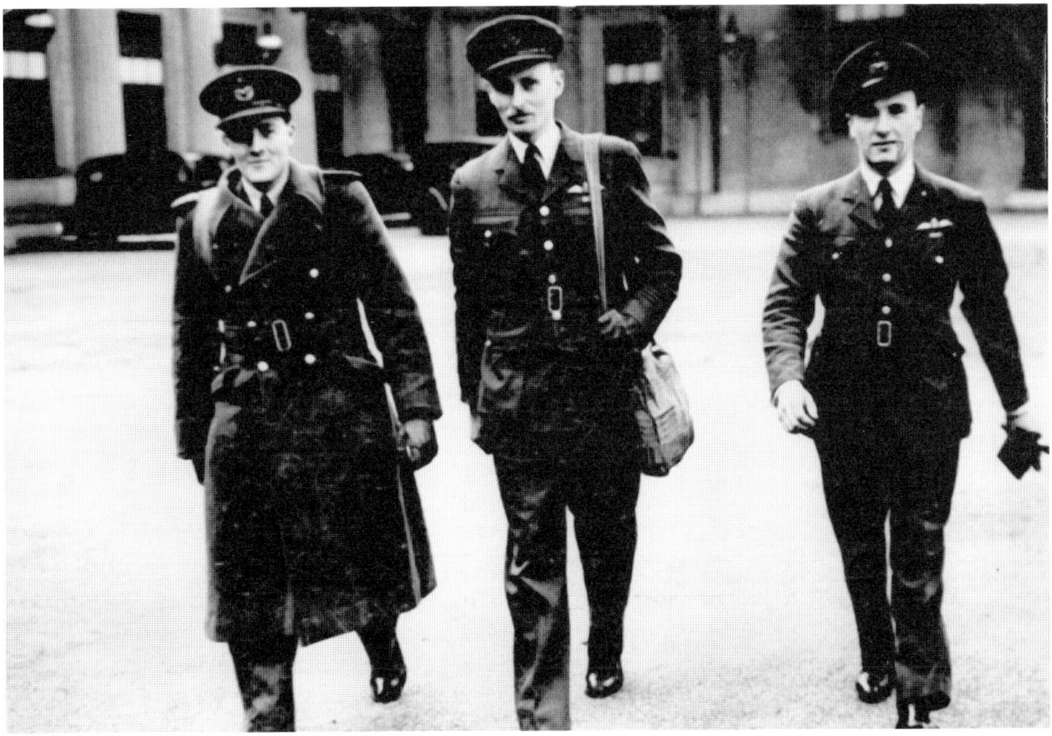

Above: Investitures were also held by the King on RAF Stations, this being one such occasion at Duxford on 16 January 1941, when certain pilots received their Battle of Britain awards. The Czechoslovak commander of 310 Squadron, Squadron Leader Sacha Hess, shakes hands with one of his flight commanders, Flight Lieutenant Jerrard Jeffries, whilst to the latter's left is 19 Squadron's Flying Officer Leonard Haines and Flight Lieutenant Jack Lawson. At extreme right is Flight Lieutenant Tom Neil, of 249 Squadron.

Opposite above: In 1958, the Battle of Britain Fighter Association was formed, membership of which was exclusively for those awarded the Battle of Britain Clasp to the 1939-45 Star. This photograph was taken at an early reunion dinner and includes many familiar faces – including guests of honour Air Chief Marshal Lord Dowding, Air Chief Marshal Sir Keith Park and Air Vice-Marshal Stanley Vincent.

Opposite below: This photograph shows members of The Battle of Britain Fighter Association in 2000. Front row, extreme right, is the Chairman, Air Chief Marshal Sir Christopher Foxley-Norris, and, again heart-warming to see the familiar faces of so many old friends. Sadly today, only one known member of The Few remains alive, namely Group Captain John 'Paddy' Hemingway, who flew Hurricanes with 85 Squadron during the Battle of Britain, and is 102 at the time of writing. It is perhaps fitting that such a photograph should conclude 'Faces of The Few'.

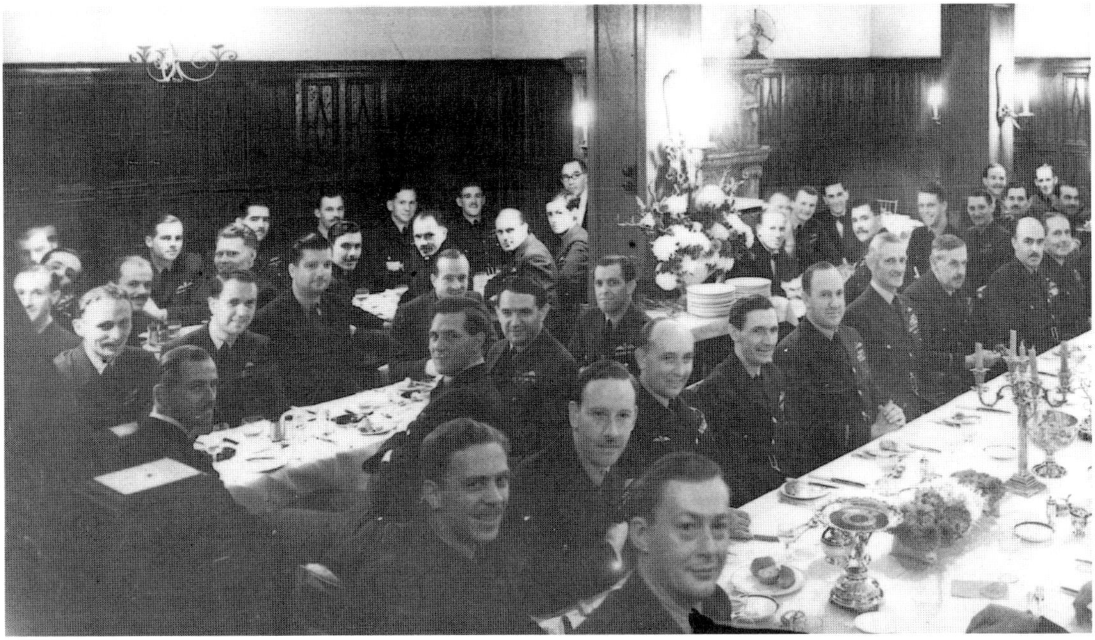

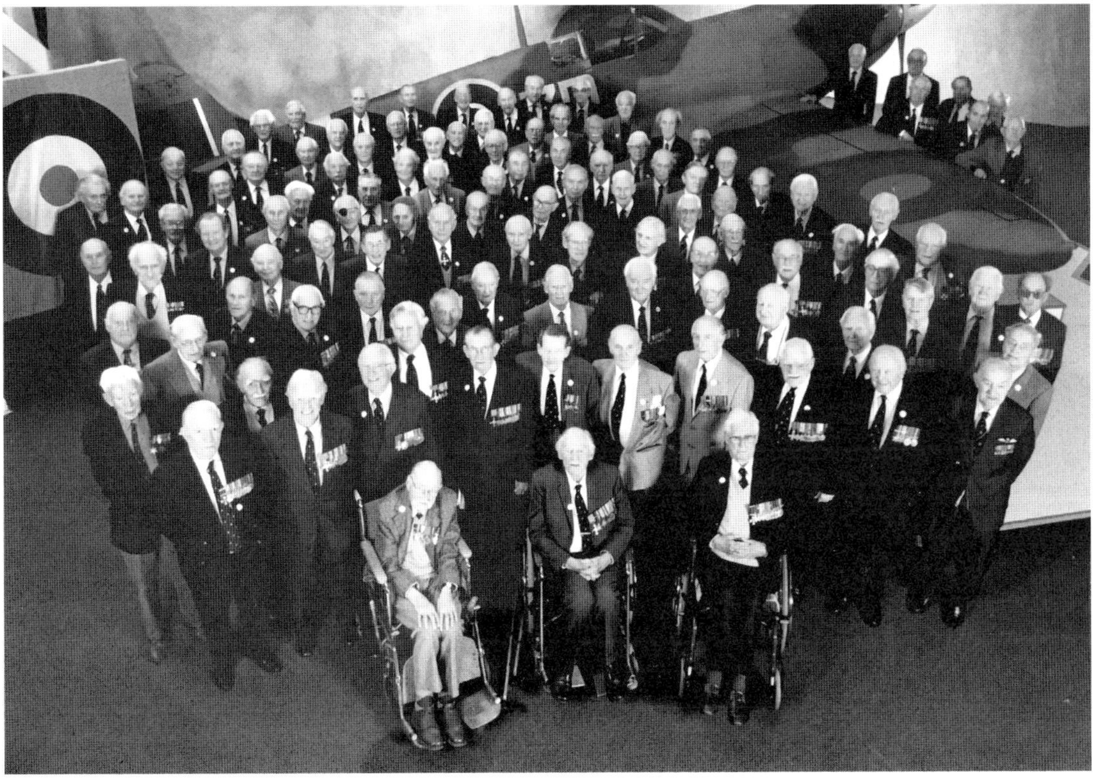

Acknowledgements

The photographs presented here have been collected over a near forty-year period, from a variety of primary sources, in the main, and over the years absorbed into my personal archive, the collation of which has provided a rich resource. Everyone, including The Few themselves, their families and fellow enthusiasts have my thanks for helping compile this collection.

In the production of this book, Martin Mace's kind help in arranging the scanning of many original images was invaluable, and, as always, the team at Pen & Sword are a pleasure to work with.

Select Bibliography

Ramsay, W (Ed), *The Battle of Britain: Then & Now*, Battle of Britain Prints International, London, 1996

Shores, C, & Williams, C, *Aces High*, Grub Street Publishing, London, 1994

Wynn, K, *Men of The Battle of Britain*, Frontline Books (Pen & Sword) Barnsley, 2015

There are also certain websites which provide information on The Few, and I would signpost readers to my own site: www.dilipsarkarauthor.com

And that run by Edward McManus of the Battle of Britain London Monument: https://bbm.org.uk

The Battle of Britain Memorial Trust is responsible for The Wing Visitor Centre and National Memorial to The Few at Capel-le-Ferne, near Folkestone and I would urge everyone to support this great cause by becoming a 'Friend of The Few': https://www.battleofbritainmemorial.org

A visit to the Kent Battle of Britain Museum is also highly recommended: http://www.kbobm.org

And The Battle of Britain Bunker Visitor Centre, including Air Vice-Marshal Park's 11 Group Operations Room: http://battleofbritainbunker.co.uk

Other Books by Dilip Sarkar

Spitfire Squadron: No 19 Squadron at War, 1939-41

The Invisible Thread: A Spitfire's Tale

Through Peril to the Stars: RAF Fighter Pilots Who Failed to Return, 1939-45

Angriff Westland: Three Battle of Britain Air Raids Through the Looking Glass

A Few of the Many: Air War 1939-45, A Kaleidoscope of Memories

Bader's Tangmere Spitfires: The Untold Story, 1941

Bader's Duxford Fighters: The Big Wing Controversy

Missing in Action: Resting in Peace?

Guards VC: Blitzkrieg 1940

Battle of Britain: The Photographic Kaleidoscope, Volumes I-IV

Fighter Pilot: The Photographic Kaleidoscope

Group Captain Sir Douglas Bader: An Inspiration in Photographs

Johnnie Johnson: Spitfire Top Gun, Part I

Johnnie Johnson: Spitfire Top Gun, Part II

Battle of Britain: Last Look Back

Spitfire! Courage & Sacrifice

Spitfire Voices: Heroes Remember

The Battle of Powick Bridge: Ambush a Fore-thought

Duxford 1940: A Battle of Britain Base at War

The Few: The Battle of Britain in the Words of the Pilots

Spitfire Manual 1940

The Sinking of HMS Royal Oak In the Words of the Survivors (re-print of Hearts of Oak)

The Last of the Few: Eighteen Battle of Britain Pilots Tell Their Extraordinary Stories

Hearts of Oak: The Human Tragedy of HMS Royal Oak

Spitfire Voices: Life as a Spitfire Pilot in the Words of the Veterans

How the Spitfire Won the Battle of Britain

Spitfire Ace of Aces: The True Wartime Story of Johnnie Johnson

Douglas Bader

Fighter Ace: The Extraordinary Life of Douglas Bader, Battle of Britain Hero (re-print of above)

Spitfire: The Photographic Biography

Hurricane Manual 1940

River Pike

The Final Few: The Last Surviving Pilots of the Battle of Britain Tell Their Stories

Arnhem 1944: The Human Tragedy of the Bridge Too Far

Spitfire! The Full Story of a Unique Battle of Britain Fighter Squadron

Battle of Britain 1940: The Finest Hour's Human Cost

Letters from The Few: Unique Memories of the Battle of Britain

Johnnie Johnson's 1942 Diary: The War Diary of the Spitfire Ace of Aces

Johnnie Johnson's Great Adventure: The Spitfire Ace of Ace's Last Look Back

Sailor Malan - Freedom Fighter: The Inspirational Story of a Spitfire Ace

Spitfire Ace of Aces – The Album: The Photographs of Johnnie Johnson

The Real Spitfire Pilot

The Real Hurricane Pilot

Bader's Big Wing Controversy: Duxford 1940.

Bader's Spitfire Wing: Tangmere 1941

Battle of Britain: The Finest Hour in Cinema

Battle of Britain: The Movie (contributor to and publisher of the now late Robert Rudhall's original edition (2000), and editor and substantial contributor to 2022 revised edition).

Spitfire Down

Forgotten Heroes of The Battle of Britain

Free French Spitfire Hero: The Diaries of and Search for Commandant Rene Mouchotte (with Jan Leeming)

The Battle of Britain on the Big Screen: The Finest Hour Through British Cinema